PETER'S SWORD

A PLAY

JACOB THOMAS VILAYIL

Translator: M C Thomas

Copyright Number TXu 2-456-719

Library of Congress LCCN: 2024920289

ISBN:979-8-218-61680-9

email: jacthomann@gmail.com

To my father~
He was a great dramatist, actor, and director.

CHARACTERS
ON STAGE

Jesus

Peter

Andrew

Judas

Thomas (Didymus)

Rest of the disciples appear as ghost characters.

Ananyas- High Priest

Eliazar- Chief Pharisee

Elihu- Priest

Asher (Roman General)

Phinehas- Roman soldier, later Centurion

Woman- all female characters embedded in one actress.

Priests

Pharisees

Soldiers

Blind man

Leper

Satan

Kids

Other Ghost characters (shadowy figures)

ACT 1 | SCENE 1

The front half of the stage is brightly lit. The rear half is pitch dark. As the soft background music gradually grows louder, light dims in synchrony in the front half of the stage. The shadow of a sword gradually rises on the curtain hanging at the rear curtain of the stage. When the shadow is halfway up, the heart-wrenching lament of a WOMAN is heard.

WOMAN

Oh, no! Slay not my child! He is my only son.

The shadow of the WOMAN appears on the curtain. A SOLDIER holding a sword menacingly also makes his appearance. The fierce lament of WOMEN rends the air. The sword rises and then falls on the WOMAN. She slumps to the ground.

WOMAN

A panic-stricken WOMAN rushes to the front stage from the rear, holding a baby and screaming for help.

Oh, God! They'll kill my child... Anyone out there to save him?!

The WOMAN rushes out through the opposite door; her shadow appears on the curtain. The slaying of the child by a SOLDIER is shown in shadow play. Loud groans and screams of WOMEN are heard.

VOICES OF WOMEN

I'm ruined! They have slayed my child! Oh Lord, why? Why have you forsaken us? Why didn't you take our lives instead?

The lamentation dies out. The background music ceases. The shadow of a WOMAN riding on a donkey, holding a swaddled baby, appears on the curtain. There is a man following them. Egyptian music in the background, Pyramids appear far in the background.

The stage gradually lights up. Holding aloft a blood-dripping sword, a young Roman SOLDIER walks in. ASHER (ROMAN GENERAL) enters from the opposite side.

ASHER (ROMAN GENERAL)

Visibly happy—

Good job!... Every obstacle is now out of the way. The king will be delighted with what we have achieved.

PHINAHAS (SOLDIER)

A threat to the king is a threat to his subjects too. The king should be defended for the nation to survive. A soldier is duty-bound to ensure that.

ASHER (ROMAN GENERAL)

You thought out a clever plan just for that. Every Jewish baby boy below the age of two has been eliminated. We have buried the next Jewish king... nay emperor.

Bowing obsequiously, PHINEHAS (SOLDIER) responds with a smile of satisfaction.

ASHER (ROMAN GENERAL)

You saved my life too. For that, you shall be rewarded. Wipe off the bloodstain from your hand.

PHINEHAS (SOLDIER) lays down the sword and wipes his bloodstained hand with a rag.

ASHER (ROMAN GENERAL) draws out the sword hanging at his waist and wipes off its bloodstains with a rag. The handle of the sword bears the emblem of the Roman Empire, and its sheath the escutcheon of his high rank.

ASHER (ROMAN GENERAL)

I hereby bestow on you the seal of my authority. It symbolizes the sovereign power of Rome. You're now my centurion and my expert advisor. Take it as a reward of recognition for the invaluable service you have rendered and as an award honoring its merit.

PHINEHAS (SOLDIER) bows, kneels, and proudly accepts the sword offered by ASHER (ROMAN GENERAL).

PHINAHAS (SOLDIER)

I thank you for this honor. No other soldier would have been offered an honor of this kind within so short a period of service.

Extremely happy, he secures the sword at his waist. He then salutes his superior in an expression of gratitude.

ASHER (ROMAN GENERAL)

Strength alone won't make a soldier; sharp mind, too, is required. An intelligent man like you won't have to draw this sword again. This sword won't smell blood nor seek it. It is a symbol of Roman power and authority.

He exits.

Light dims and then brightens intermittently. The shadow of pyramids once again appears on the rear curtain. Music flows softly.

The shadow of a boy riding a donkey appears on the curtain. Accompanying him are a man and a woman. They now move in the opposite direction from where they moved before. The pyramids recede from them.

As the light fades, the music grows louder, reaches a crescendo, and then subsides. The choir sings a hymn that evokes change, progress, and expectations.

SCENE 2

The front half of the stage is dimly lit. Shadow of a multitude appears on the curtain, accompanied by screams, yells, and curses.

CROWD

Enforce the Law of Moses, Stone her to death!

A man drags a woman and throws her in front of the CROWD. She falls prostrate on the ground. The stage slowly lights up. JESUS, PETER, JUDAS, and THOMAS enter from one side. PETER alone walks close to JESUS. When they reach the center of the stage, PETER stops and turns back, squinting suspiciously. The other disciples move back and stand together at one side. JESUS is in the middle of the stage. The hapless woman is now seen sitting on the ground, her head drooped. The veil covering her head has partially fallen off. Her clothes are torn, and her hair disheveled, suggesting she has been dragged. Brandishing a bone, one from the CROWD rushes out and kicks her.

THE MAN

She has committed adultery. We are going to enforce the Law of Moses on her. There is no one here who will speak for her.

Scoffingly to Jesus—

Oh, you compassionate and all-knowing master, what do you say? She guilty? What do you think should be done to her?

JESUS sits on the ground, studying the woman's face with keen and compassionate attention. He rises and looks at the CROWD.

JESUS

What punishment does the Law of Moses prescribe for her?

A yelling CROWD armed with stones moves menacingly toward the woman covers half the stage, which is visualized in such a way as to present a synchronized display of shadows, images, light, and darkness.

THE CROWD

Death by stoning!

JESUS

Don't you know that, as per the Law of Moses, one should not covet the wealth or property of others? Is it not adulterous to look lecherously at a woman?

A stone falls beside Jesus. It unsettles PETER and the other disciples. They step back. Light falls upon the COMMANDER, PHINAHAS (SOLDIER), a ANANYAS (HIGH PRIEST), ELIHU THE PRIEST, a high-ranking Pharisee, a few priests and Pharisees. The spotlight shifts to the woman. Her comely face is now visible to all. JESUS picks up a stone.

JESUS

Could she have committed adultery all by herself? What about her partners in the sin? Shouldn't they also be stoned to death as per the Law of Moses? If you want to enforce the law, shouldn't you do so justly and impartially?

The CROWD becomes restive. JESUS sits on the ground and, with his raised index finger, scribbles on the ground. The audience is not able to see what he is scribbling. The light falls on the COMMANDER, priests, and Pharisees.

Lost in thought, JESUS scribbles more, taking his own time.

The CROWD keeps clamoring for the women's punishment.

The Spotlight shifts to the ANANYAS (HIGH PRIEST), revealing the cruel expression on his face. The light falls on him as he angrily pushes people aside and emerges into full view.

The light follows the COMMANDER as he emerges from the dark and joins the ANANYAS (HIGH PRIEST).

The other priests and the Pharisees exit hastily.

The light now shifts to PETER and the other disciples. PETER's face is slowly overspread by dismay. The clamor dies down. The anger of the CROWD subsides.

Stones slip down from people's hands and fall to the ground. The CROWD disperses. A few appear as gloomy shadows.

JESUS sits in front of the woman under focused light.

The woman raises her head and looks at JESUS, her eyes pleading for mercy and pardon. She is exhausted. Her face is bruised. JESUS looks into her eyes.

JESUS

Is your name Loruhamah? There is nothing in creation that will be denied God's mercy. Your accusers are gone. Never mind your past. I don't condemn you. You are a child of God. Sin no more. Make a new beginning. Have a grip on your mind just as strongly as your dress has on your body. Submission is not a woman's destiny. Get up. Go back to life.

JESUS gets up and moves away. With brightened faces, the disciples follow him. The lights fade out. When the lights return, the COMMANDER, ANANYAS (HIGH PRIEST), and their entourage are left on the stage.

ANANYAS (HIGH PRIEST)

It was a ploy that we worked very hard on —didn't have the least idea he'd turn the tables on us, and she would get away so cheap. What a terrible loss of face!

COMMANDER

True, the woman got away just like that, but there was a point in what he said. She could not have committed adultery by herself alone. Those who used her and those who acted as pimps between them and her are equally guilty. Why should someone pointing that out bring shame on us? I don't feel humiliated in any way. I only feel embarrassed that it did not occur to me before He pointed it out.

Looks quizzically at the ANANYAS (HIGH PRIEST)—

ANANYAS (HIGH PRIEST)

Better keep your homilies to yourself! I don't care if you're a Roman soldier. My tongue is itching. If it lashes out, you will see stars... A deluded carpenter who claims to be the Messiah has insulted me enough.

The ANANYAS (HIGH PRIEST) and the PHARISEES look on curiously.

Phew! Phony Messiah!

Light fades out. When it returns, PETER is seen standing with the other two disciples. JESUS and the other disciples appear as shadows.

PETER

They laid a trap for the master, but he outsmarted them.

THOMAS

What was it that Master scribbled on the ground? The name of some woman or place?

PETER

Barging in—

It was the name of some woman, for sure. Rahab is what he wrote— she is pretty historical.

THOMAS and JUDAS react skeptically to PETER's sudden act of wisdom.

JUDAS

I couldn't get you. Who are you speaking about?

THOMAS

He must have asked the master and found out.

PETER

The master chose to speak not a word as though he was under the vow of silence. He was lost in contemplation. Thank goodness he could sidestep the trap and save the life of a poor woman. How embarrassing! Even after being with him for so long, you failed to read his mind!

The lights fade out. When they come on, the previous scene returns.

THE COMMANDER

To the ANANYAS (HIGH PRIEST)

Rahab is the name of a woman. Does it ring a bell?

THE ANANYAS (HIGH PRIEST)

It does; it's the name of the first prostitute mentioned in the Bible. The owner of the first red street in history. Look her up in the Book of Joshua. She helped the Jews to conquer Jericho city. Because of her feat, she was saved from certain death.

THE COMMANDER

All the more reason for us not to feel piqued.

THE ANANYAS (HIGH PRIEST)

Hold on!

In a hushed tone—

She was the great-grandmother of King David.

THE OTHERS shudder hearing it.

THE OTHERS

What! The great-grandmother of our beloved King David?

The background music grows louder as the lights dim in synchrony.

The voice from above echoing, "Offsprings of prostitutes! Offsprings of prostitutes!"

SCENE 3

JESUS enters, followed by PETER, ANDREW, THOMAS, and JUDAS. A possessed WOMAN is screaming and thrashing about on the floor center stage. She sees JESUS when the light dawns.

THE WOMAN

Screaming—

There you are once again! Why do you come after me?

She switches to pleading.

Have mercy on me, Son of David! Please cast out the devil from me!

She resumes her reviling.

Get off! Touch me not! Why do you torment me? Be off!

JESUS

If you want to be healed, say, "Please cast out the devil from me."

THE WOMAN

Grant me freedom from this devil, Oh Son of David!

Switching suddenly to a roar—

Where will I go if you drive me out of her? Show me a place if you want me to leave her.

JESUS

I shall not touch you.

JESUS takes the staff from PETER and holds it toward the WOMAN.

Hold on to it!

Loudly and Sternly—

Get out, Satan, from this daughter of Abraham!

The WOMAN falls on the ground as though cast down. She thrashes about. A devilish howl can be heard from the back. Light fades out.

SCENE 4

The brightness of light on the stage increases steadily. Satan's shadow looms on the curtain. Simultaneously, the shadow of JESUS also emerges on the curtain. JESUS sits down on the floor. The music keeps rising and falling. The view of a desert appears on the curtain. SATAN enters the stage.

SATAN

He is holding some fruits.

You are now dead, hungry, and thirsty. Have your fill of these fruits. What else can you find in this desert? Surely, you won't reject my offer.

JESUS

If the same desert could once supply quails and water from rock to the people of Israel, I can find sustenance in the Word of God that speaks of it. Only those who have mastered the brutal cravings of the mouth and the stomach will have the strength to face the world. Job didn't succumb to your torments, temptations, and threats, and now you want to try your tricks with the Son of Man?

SATAN

I shall give you all the riches of the world if you submit yourself to me.

JESUS

They are not yours to give! The riches of the world belong to my Father in Heaven, who created the earth and the riches therein. How can you then offer them to me? True, they were given to you once, but you forfeited them when you became conceited and rebellious. It was not to be a slave to the world that I fasted for forty days in this desert but to master them. To master the world is to master oneself.

SATAN

Say what you will. The fact is that all these are mine to give or to keep as I please. I alone exercise authority over this world. I shall give all of that to you if you become my follower. For a fleeting moment, bow down and worship me; you shall be the ruler of multitude of nations. I shall also serve you and safeguard you forever.

JESUS

Begone, Satan! Thirst for power and authority is a human weakness. Overcoming it is next to impossible. Anyone who acquires power and authority gets so addicted to it that he won't be able to come out of its vicious grip. Thus enslaved, he'll go wherever it leads him like a slave following his master's shadow. You have enticed the whole world with your wile and guile. You have injected corruption into this world. In the pursuit of power, nations and empires fight unto self-destruction. And you have enough malevolent delight watching it. You sneaked into the Garden of Eden and enticed the first woman to disobey God's command. You hide behind darkness. Look in the mirror and see how ugly you are. This world hasn't seen anything as revolting as you.

SATAN

My appearance doesn't matter to me at all. Why should it matter to you? Power and authority are all that matter in this world. You think you can save the world by not knowing how it works. Join hands with me, and I shall show you how you can achieve anything you wish.

JESUS

You tried this trick on Adam and Eve. You won. They lost, lost their heavenly paradise. I have come to retake possession of that paradise and restore it to the children of Adam and Eve.

SATAN

I challenge you to show me anyone who does not hanker after power, authority, and riches. Humanity is hopelessly addicted to them. Liberating them is next to impossible. That is the truth. Now, you face the truth.

JESUS

I have come with a mission to make the impossible possible.

SATAN

Laughing derisively—

If I could enter the Garden of Eden, so can I every other paradise on Earth. My agents will establish, maintain, and secure my authority over all the earth. All your efforts will be in vain, just like your father's.

He exits guffawing—

SCENE 5

Light falls on the front half of the stage. Background music begins aloud and gradually softens. The shadow of a well appears on the curtain. A WOMAN dressed as a Samarian enters the front half of the stage carrying a pitcher. She ambles across.

JESUS enters.

JESUS

Woman, I'm thirsty. Would you give me some water?

THE WOMAN

Visibly unnerved—

How can you, a Jew, ask me, a Samaritan woman, for water? Maddened by thirst, you're breaking an important Jewish taboo.

JESUS

All the water in this desert comes from one and the same source. It doesn't discriminate between Jews and Samaritans.

THE WOMAN

You may draw water from the well and drink. According to the faith of our fathers, this is Jacob's well. And so, it's yours too.

JESUS

If you drink this water, you'll feel thirsty again, but I can give you water to quench your thirst once and for all.

WOMEN

Studies Jesus skeptically—

But you said you are thirsty. You asked me for a drink. Now, you say you can give me the water to quench my thirst forever! Drink the water you have and give me some too.

Smiling mischievously—

It will save me the bother of having to visit this well. We believe that, at the request of Moses, God provided water in the desert to our ancestors during their exodus from Egypt. Are you a prophet of the line of Moses?

JESUS

I had taken you for a sorceress, but now I know you're a wise and intelligent woman.

THE WOMAN

We hold fast to the belief of our ancestors that our redeemer, Thayeb, will come again and take us into the fold of God's chosen ones and will make us worthy of worshipping Him along with the Jews.

JESUS

Watching the woman in poignant affection for her—

You're now speaking to someone greater than Thayeb; You're speaking to the redeemer who has come to save the Jews.

THE WOMAN

Then your name should be Joshua.

JESUS

Yes, that is my name.

THE WOMAN

If you're indeed Joshua, you're our redeemer too. I trust you'll make us a part of the Jewish nation. I'll go and bring my husband and relatives to receive together the redemption you offer.

JESUS

Husband, you said. But you have been married to five men, and the one you are now living with is not really your husband. You kept them all under your control, practicing sorcery. You are taking water from this well now to use it for your next episode of sorcery.

THE WOMAN

You're indeed God's prophet. The Israelites will never accept us as
their own. They deny us even the right to enter the Jerusalem Temple
and pray in it. They keep us out, counting us worse than the gentiles.

JESUS

God does not reside in Jerusalem or on mountains. Fill your mind
with wholesome thoughts. Free yourself from the hold of worldly
aspirations. Submit yourself, body and soul, to God. Then, you will
become, yourself, the temple of God. It'll bring you abiding peace.
And you'll thirst no more.

THE WOMAN

Thank you, Master, for bringing us the hope of redemption.

JESUS

I shall send you an all-powerful helper who'll fight for your cause
and bring you under a new covenant to fulfill your hopes.

THE WOMAN

I shall go and announce to my people the salvation you have
brought.

The WOMAN exits. Light fades out.

SCENE 6

When light comes on, seen on the stage are the COMMANDER, a ANANYAS (HIGH PRIEST), a CENTURION, and ELIHU THE PRIEST.

ANANYAS (HIGH PRIEST)

Yet another of our game plans has flopped. What next? If only we could win over one of his disciples, we might discover the secret of his power.

COMMANDER

Even for his disciples, he is a riddle. They, themselves, might be wondering who he really is: an impostor, a magician, the Son of God, or, as we believe, an agent of Beelzebub, the ruler of hell.

CENTURION

I have devised a scheme that makes use of magic, chants, and guile to trap him.

He takes out a coin from under his garment.

PRIEST

Amazed—

What! Are you going to trap him using a coin?

CENTURION

This coin bears the seal of Rome's power. All the subjects of Rome are bound to use it.

ANANYAS (HIGH PRIEST)

Great idea! He and his disciples don't pay tax to Rome. We can use that to trap him and accuse him of treason. Soon, he will be on his way to jail.

JESUS enters. The disciples stand together to one side of the stage. Only one or two are clearly visible. A SENIOR PHARISEE walks in. He surveys the others on the stage.

SENIOR PHARISEE

Addressing Jesus—

Is it right to divorce one's wife?

JESUS

It is unlawful to divorce a woman whom you have married with God
as witness.

SENIOR PHARISEE

Is the Law of Moses wrong then?

JESUS

Moses and the prophets will never ask us to do anything wrong;
instead, Moses has only presented a way out to women to escape the
ruination of their bodies and souls at the hands of their heartless
tormentors. The degradation of women is the assured shortcut to the
degeneration of society.

PRIEST

Comes forward, tosses a coin, and catches it.

What do you make of this?

JESUS

A coin made of a metal mined from the earth. It will lose its value
and be returned to the earth in the course of time.

CENTURION

Are you prophesying that the Roman Empire, whose seal it bears,
will also one day become mere earth?

JESUS

You have answered your own question. No empire lasts forever. None have. None will.

SENIOR PHARISEE

So, that will surely mean that we should not accept subjection by that authority? Are you then suggesting that we should not pay tax to Rome?

JESUS

Give to each what he deserves, to Caesar what is Caesar's, and to God what is God's.

How terrible for you, priests! For the sake of this coin, you choose to be defenders of Rome and devotees of Caesar. You have, by that, sinned against the First Commandment.

PRIEST

With fearful apprehension—

How can we even think of such a thing?

JESUS

You have placed your hope and trust in this coin, not realizing it carries the image of Caesar. Is that not idolatry? You're acting just like your forefather, Aaron. When Moses descended Mount Sinai carrying the tablets of the Ten Commandments, he exploded at the sight he saw—Aaron was leading the people in the worship of a golden calf, a clear violation of the very first of the commandments he was carrying. In a blaze of righteous indignation, Moses threw the tablets onto the ground, shattering them into pieces. Fortunately, his brother Aaron escaped his wrath, but God punished his kin. You're repeating what he did. Love for riches is making you commit idolatry by living in acceptance of this coin. You have legitimized the worship of images. And you claim to be the priests of Yahweh! In the line of Moses!

Pause

Don't you priests realize that by paying tax to Rome, you're contributing to empire-building, the spread of slavery, and the oppression of the powerless, besides helping build temples for their pagan gods? By that, you're also guilty of idolatry and repeated violation of the First Law of Moses. How can you still claim to be the priests of Yahweh?! You're, in fact, priests of Baal. Well, even your costumes too resemble theirs!

Pause

How terrible for you, priests! You have shut your doors to God's prophets. Like magicians, you take recourse to the occult. You hold *Urim* and *Thummim* close to your heart. Casting them like dice, you use them to prophesy. Like sorcerers, you fleece gullible people, proffering them prophesies. You arrogate to yourself the power and authority of the prophets. As if that wasn't bad enough, you smuggled brass idols from Egypt and offered them to the people for worship. You clamor, 'The temple of Yahweh! The temple of Yahweh!' but your idol worship reduces it to the temple of Baal. I tell you, it'll be razed to the ground. No stone on stone will be left standing in it, and foxes and crawling creatures will make its ruins their abode. God is light and radiates light, but you walk in darkness. Your hearts are dark caverns. From the Garden of Eden to this day, you worship serpents. The cunning serpent resides in your hearts, stratagems to lead others astray. Have you not heard Yahweh proclaim through the prophets: *Ignorance is destroying my people? They make their living by the sins of my people. I desire their annihilation.* Beware, priests; the miseries of the people will fall on you too. Their blood will be required of you. You humor the king and his nobles with wickedness and deception. This day, I counsel you, sow justice, and reap mercy. Stop your wrongdoings and set your hearts on Yahweh, the Most Gracious. Remember the Day of Judgment and avoid God's consuming wrath.

Light fades—

SCENE 7

*JESUS and his disciples THOMAS DIDYMUS, PETER, and
ANDREW enter from one side of the stage. ELIZER, the head of
the Pharisees, two other Pharisees, ELIHU THE PRIEST, and a
PRIEST enter from the other side.*

PRIEST

You and your disciples are disregarding the Law of Moses. You do not
observe the Sabbath.

JESUS

Oh, priests, if you indeed belong to the tribe of Levi, how can you
forget the deeds of your ancestors that violated both these codes of
the Law of Moses! Didn't they take part in the celebratory procession
Joshua led in Jericho City on a Sabbath day? Does not the Law of
Moses forbid you from fighting in wars, even preparing for it? You
conveniently forget the help they offered to Judas Maccabee in the
preparations for war. How terrible for you, Levitical priests! Moses

has given you no rights at all in Israel. You have instead been given the duty to look after the temple and perform its rituals. Ignoring that, you go after idol worship. Your priesthood is not everlasting, nor are your rights.

The PRIESTS whisper in each other's ears. The PHARISEES depart in the same direction they came from. Seeing them go, the PRIESTS follow them.

JESUS

To the disciples—

You are called to be children of light, so walk in the light. Be on your guard against the wily serpent. He is the devil incarnate. He has led humanity astray, and he's ever on the prowl to do that.

THOMAS DIDYMUS

Master, reveal to us the secrets of this world.

JESUS

It will be revealed to you in due course.

JESUS whispers in THOMAS DIDYMUS' ears, who is amazed at what he hears.

PETER AND ANDREW

To Thomas Didymus —

Please reveal to us the secret JESUS shared with you.

THOMAS DIDYMUS

If I reveal to you the truths Jesus told me, stone will turn into double-edged swords and slay you to death.

Pause

They're beyond your grasp. Why I am chosen to be its bearer, I know not, how terribly fortunate I am!

The curtain falls.

ACT II | SCENE I

The shadow of a large crowd is seen displayed on the back curtain. The hubbub of children grows louder.

In the front half of the stage are JESUS, PETER, ANDREW, THOMAS DIDYMUS, and JUDAS. They are standing in full view of the audience.

JESUS seats himself on a rock. A little boy wades his way through the crowd toward JESUS.

PETER tries to stop the boy with his staff.

The lights progressively brighten the stage.

JESUS

To Peter—

Why do you prevent the child from coming to me, Peter? Let him.

PETER withdraws his staff. The child comes near JESUS and fixes his eyes on the former's face. His face radiates a wonderous joy.

JESUS

Do you see the radiance on the face of this child, Peter? That's the radiance with which God's first creations shone. Sin has not entered him.

Pause

Until man sinned at the behest of the devil, God's creation radiated the innocence of such children.

Pause

Remember this: you shall not enter the Kingdom of Heaven unless you become like little children.

The disciples look at each other in dismay. The child sits in JESUS' lap and rubs his fingers through his beard.

JESUS

Those who cause these innocent children to stumble shall incur damnation. The next generation will be ruined if their innocence is soiled. Give them all the care they need until they become capable of distinguishing the good from the bad. Suffer them, and they will find out the truth. Take care that their needs are not neglected. Supplement their diet with honey and yogurt. Nurture them in love.

JUDAS

In subdued tone—

God had promised Israel to provide honey and milk in Canaan. When did that milk turn sour?

PETER

The master is speaking exactly like Isaiah.

JESUS

Tell me, Peter, from whom do the rulers of the world collect taxes, from their children or from others?

PETER

From others, of course.

JESUS

Would you give the food meant for your children to dogs instead? You won't. How much more is your heavenly Father mindful of your needs? These are the children of light. Do everything needed to preserve the luminous innocence of their faces. Cause it not to dim or vanish. The days of those who lead them astray are numbered. Condemnation will descend on them like a double-edged sword. Children are the gatekeepers of Heaven. The keys of Heaven are in their safekeeping. Watch out! Be on your guard against the devil lying in wait to snatch them away. Be you also as pure and free as they are.

MYSTERIOUS VOICE

Echoing—

Children are the gatekeepers of Heaven. With them are the Heaven's keys. Turn back and become like them. Children alone are the light of the world.

The lights fade out.

SCENE 2

In the front half of the stage are JESUS and the DISCIPLES,
standing. Light falls on them. The shadow of a LEPER appears on
the rear curtain. These figures slowly move toward the front of the
stage. In a while, the LEPER appears on the stage.

PEOPLE

At the top of their voice—

Get away, you unclean and accursed man! You're blocking the way of
the holy ones. See, you're reaping the wages of your sins. Sins breed
leprosy. Your place is outside the city; how dare you come here? Why
aren't you dead? Death alone is the remedy for you.

LEPER

Face covered—

Son of David, take pity on me and heal me; I, too, am a child of Abraham. Oh! Son of David.

JESUS

If you truly believe that you're a child of Abraham, then redemption is at hand for you.

JESUS stretches out his hand and removes the cloth covering the leper's face. He puts his hand on his head. The disciples look on, shocked.

Look, your faith has cleansed you.

The LEPER stands transfixed for a moment, then slumps to the floor screaming.

JESUS retreats from him a few steps. In the meantime, someone pushes a BLIND MAN toward him.

Feeling his way with a stick, the blind man hobbles closer to Jesus.

THE BLIND MAN

Cure me of my blindness, O Jesus of Nazareth. Cast a ray of light on my eyes. May the radiance of your face give life to my eyes. Grant me the fortune to behold the Messiah.

JESUS lays his hands on the blind man's shoulders. He then sits down, spits on the ground, makes a paste with his spittle and mud, and anoints the man's eyes with the paste.

JESUS

Go and wash your face in the pool of Siloam. From there, go to your
kith and kin and tell them all that has happened.

Pause

Your blindness is easy to cure, but there are some whose blindness is
impossible to cure.

Looking dazed, the blind man exits.

PETER

Stepping forward—

Please, Master, tell us who they are, whose blindness cannot be
cured. How wonderful it would be if a cure for cataracts could be
revealed, from which people everywhere in the world may get relief.

JESUS

It is extremely difficult to drive away darkness that spreads from a
corrupted body to the mind and to the soul. They have sight but not
vision. They have ears but not the power to hear. They walk in a
world of light but see nothing.

PETER

Save me from such a bad state, Master.

JESUS

Focus your inner eye, Peter, and find escape from the world of illusions. There is a knowledge that transcends the five senses. That alone is worthwhile, abiding knowledge. You have been blinded by the illusions of the world. The arrogance and greed they bring make people blind in their minds. You can measure ignorance using knowledge. No measuring rod avails for gauging illusory perception aright. The ability to do so is the secret of spiritual maturity. That is when you will cease to be the impetuous Simon and become steadfast, unwavering Peter.

PETER looks dolefully at JESUS, wiping the tears welling up in his eyes.

THOMAS

To Andrew—

Why did the master not cure the cataract in Peter's eye?

ANDREW

Worldly assumptions are the essence of his blindness. His eyes will open only when he acquires real knowledge.

THOMAS

As for me, knowledge is not of great interest to me. So long as I don't go blind, I am all right.

SCENE 3

The ANANYAS (HIGH PRIEST) is lost in thought. The image of a temple appears on the rear curtain. The ELIAZAR (CHIEF PHARISEE), ELIHU, the ANANYAS (HIGH PRIEST), and two other Pharisees enter.

ELIAZAR (CHIEF PHARISEE)

Greetings to you!

ANANYAS (HIGH PRIEST)

Bitterly—

Keep your blooming greetings to yourself. I hear things that I should never have heard; I see things that I should never have seen. Mark my words; evil days are surely upon us.

ELIAZAR (CHIEF PHARISEE)

I have made inquiries about it and cannot help but share your anxieties and apprehensions.

He points to the outside.

And to confirm them, I have also brought him.

ANANYAS (HIGH PRIEST)

Who's there?

A soldier enters.

Soldier, a man is waiting outside. Bring him in.

A blind man gets pushed inside. He stumbles but steadies himself and comes to a halt. He looks baffled.

ANANYAS (HIGH PRIEST)

Is it true that you were previously blind?

BLINDMAN

Feebly and apprehensively—

Yes, I was born blind. My parents and relatives will vouch you that I was.

ANANYAS (HIGH PRIEST)

A blind man gaining sight just like that is simply unheard of.

BLINDMAN

Jesus of Nazareth gave sight to me. He is indeed the long-awaited
Messiah.

ANANYAS (HIGH PRIEST)

Don't jump to conclusions yet. You don't have to teach me the
scriptures. We know the

tribe and the town where the Messiah will be born.

BLINDMAN

Submissively—

Pardon me, sir, but I, who was blind, can see now, but you, who have
sight, can't see what is in front of you. The blind see, the deaf hear,
the lame walk, and lepers are healed all because of him. But you shut
your eyes and pretend not to have seen all that. But, I cannot deny
the blessings I have received from Jesus.

THE ELIAZAR (CHIEF PHARISEE)

Drawing out a dagger from his waist and holding it menacingly.

This dagger will test and prove the real power of the vision you
regained!

BLINDMAN

Trembling with fear—

Oh, no. Spare me! My eyes are swirling! I can't see anything!

He falls to the ground.

The lights fade out.

SCENE 4

JESUS is seen with his DISCIPLES, center stage. It is all very quiet.

JESUS

Who do you think I am?

PETER

You're the Messiah, the Son of the living God.

JESUS

Simon Caiaphas, you did not receive this from anyone born of a woman. You received it directly from the Holy Spirit. Keep it, all of you, a secret. It is to be revealed only to those whom my Father chooses when the time comes.

PETER

Supporting himself on his staff—

As you say, master.

JESUS

Addressing his disciples—

Peter, you speak as prompted by your bodily self. Do not like the Pharisees who go and sit in the front row.

He takes the staff from Peter.

I give you a staff and shawl only. As Moses and David were shepherds, be shepherds of the people. Don't be anxious about what to wear, what to eat, and what to say. God is faithful and will provide for your needs. Do not worry about what to say when confronted or cornered. The Holy Spirit will give you the words for such occasions.

He surveys everyone

I shall reveal to you everything from the beginning of the world to its end. You'll be the messengers of a new vision... a new gospel. Sow the seeds of love without expecting to reap its harvest. In loving one another dwells the essence of the law and the prophets. Build houses for God on the foundation of love. Allow God to abide in your body and soul. Let the urgings and energy of the divine energy in you bear fruit abundantly. Rise like the sun and shine. You're hallowed by the radiance of Yahweh. You have been called to proclaim peace, to spread goodness, and to bring redemption to the people.

Light fades—

SCENE 5

JESUS and the DISCIPLES: surrounding them, a crowd. The light falls on their faces. The shadow of a huge crowd appears on the back curtain. The ANANYAS (HIGH PRIEST), ELIHU, and the ELIAZAR (CHIEF PHARISEE) enter the stage in the company of a few other PHARISEES. The DISCIPLES move to the side to make way for them.

ANANYAS (HIGH PRIEST)

To Jesus—

Who has given you the authority to violate the law of Moses? You have belittled Jewish ritual practices. On what basis do you do that? And by what authority?

ELIAZAR (CHIEF PHARISEE)

You and your disciples do not observe the Sabbath, which you are commanded to do. Your disciples do not wash their hands before eating. You eat in the company of those, the Israelites keep aloof from, like the tax collectors, sinners, and those who are forbidden to visit the temple.

JESUS

Regarding them thoughtfully for a brief while and then saying with gentle firmness—

You observe the Laws of Moses, but I observe the laws of the God who gave Moses those laws.

ANANYAS (HIGH PRIEST)

If you're obeying the Laws of God, give us a sign for it so that we, too, may believe in you and obey your laws.

JESUS

You hypocrites, why do you test the Lord again and again? Have you forgotten the Lord who fed you with manna and quails in the desert and led you to Canaan, the land of promise? The sign I shall give you are these words of God: Mene mene tekel.

ANANYAS (HIGH PRIEST) AND ELIAZAR (CHIEF PHARISEE)

Startled—

Mene mene tekel...

Turn to each other.

A HEAVENLY VOICE

Mene mene tekel upharsin.

Lights fade and then brighten in synch with the rising and dipping chant

SCENE 6

The Shadow of one of the entrances of the Jerusalem Temple appears on the back curtain. JESUS is addressing the audience seated in the front rows.

JESUS

Sons and daughters of Jerusalem, prepare yourself for the day of judgment. You seek me because you have eaten your fill. Those who are hungry will be fed, and those who are thirsty will get water to drink. Yet your hunger and thirst will remain. Neither the body nor the world offers permanence. But the water I'll give will quench the thirst of your soul unto eternity. To the despised, the desolate, and those who fear the Lord, I shall bring redemption. Why do you spend your hard earnings on things that promise momentary satisfaction? In this world, every satisfaction is a prelude to dissatisfaction. Listen carefully to my words and attain the enduring joy of life in its fullness. Let the evil man shed his sinful ways and the dishonest man his treacheries. Turn to God and live.

The ANANYAS (HIGH PRIEST) enters looking grave and indignant in the company of other PRIESTS and PHARISEES.

PRIEST

Addressing Jesus—

You have desecrated the temple of God.

ANANYAS (HIGH PRIEST)

You have dishonored the holy house of God. You slighted the priesthood, broke our cherished traditions, and devalued the Sabbath.

Furious—

With what authority are you doing all this?

JESUS

How's that you use the holy temple of Yahweh to grant pardon to mean and evil men for a price? Why do you perform animal sacrifices for them and take a share of the oblation? You're neither mindful of nor concerned about sinful transgression.

Don't you belong to the tribe of Levi, to which Yahweh gave no other privilege than to act as his ritual priests? But you take a big chunk of the offerings made to God as your share.

ANANYAS (HIGH PRIEST)

We are duty-bound to ensure the inviolability and sanctity of the house of Yahweh. Nothing abominable will be permitted in it.

JESUS

You may be the heirs of Aaron, but only Herod, who built this temple, has a claim on it. How can you then go around calling it the temple of Yahweh? You glorify Herod's name like you do Yahweh's name. You also look upon him as your master. Whose abode is this temple really, Yahweh's or Babel's?

ANANYAS (HIGH PRIEST)

Herod built this temple strictly in accordance with our religious needs and plans and handed it over to us. To us, this is the house of our God.

JESUS

Yes, yes, he also performed its dedication sprinkled with the blood of the Chief Priest. You, priests, are so good at pretending piety in front of the people. But your heart is frothing with viper venom. You want premium seats at feasts and to be greeted on the streets with reverence. You bedazzle people with your glittering and ponderous religious attire. You have reduced prayer and fasting to a theater of hypocrisy. You're fastidious about keeping the temple's vessels and burnishing its brass fittings, but you pay no attention to the dirt that has accumulated in your hearts. You have thus become whitened sepulchres that reek of rotten corpses.

PRIESTS

How dare you question the laws and traditions handed down by our forefathers?

JESUS

You have forgotten that our father Jacob had said that the swords
wielded by Simon and Levi were weapons of adventure. He has by
that transferred the rights of the tribe of Levi to Joseph's sons,
Manasseh and Ephraim. You shall die by your sword.

Pause

You distance yourself from society and turn a blind eye to the needs
of widows and destitute. You prescribe penitential sacrifices for sins
and charge exorbitant fees for performing them. You, priests,
collaborate with the Pharisees who teach the Laws of Moses and
directions of Aaron and agree with the Sadducees who argue that
there is no afterlife. You have joined hands with the Pharisees to
seize the houses of widows. When it comes to contracts that confer
authority, you're with the Sadducees, and when it comes to financial
matters, you're with the Pharisees. How on Earth can you then lay
claim to the legacy of Aaron and Levi?

ANDREW

Prescribing law after law, they themselves became the law.

JUDAS

Prescribing laws can be quite a lucrative business. Mathew will
attest to that.

PETER

The master was speaking of those who prescribe fake laws.

JESUS

After a short pause—

Beware of the leaven of the priestly class!

ANDREW

To Peter and Judas

From when did the priests get into the business of selling leaven?

PETER

What the master referred is not that.

ANDREW and JUDAS look suspiciously at PETER.

JUDAS

What the master said about the priestly class is indeed very true.
They and the Pharisees have conspired to become the established
connoisseurs of leaven. Their approval is needed to certify the
effectiveness of leaven.

Sighing—

Ghosh! They use that, too, as an avenue to make money!

In a whisper—

Our purse is empty—they pluck money from the air!

JESUS

You, priests, do charity as a show in front of crowds. You gather people with trumpet calls. You want to be called Rabi without at all deserving it. You adorn your cloaks with tassels.

To a priest—

Great priest Melchizedek is an icon of justice; you misuse his name to claim riches that you don't deserve. Greed has become a mental illness with you. You exact your pound of flesh even from poor widows. Your ritual chants are of no greater worth than the rattling of latches. You have no idea what your chants mean, nor do you care to understand.

ANANYAS (HIGH PRIEST)

You're denigrating priesthood and our anointed ancestors.

JESUS

Furious—

Tell me if Elohim, the Lord you proclaim, is singular or plural in form. If you give me the right answer, I shall admit that priesthood has been rightly handed down to you.

Caught off guard, the PRIESTS and PHARISEES turn to each other, gesturing for an answer.

PETER and the other disciples look aghast at each other.

The PRIESTS, PHARISEES, and their entourage swiftly exit, casting angry glances at JESUS—Lights fade out.

SCENE 7

The stage is dimly lit. People crisscross the stage. When the stage is fully lit, the ANANYAS (HIGH PRIEST) and the ELIAZAR (CHIEF PHARISEE) are seen ambling onto the stage.

ELIAZAR (CHIEF PHARISEE)

Didn't you hear what the Sadducees, theologians, and other spiritual men said?

ANANYAS (HIGH PRIEST)

Vehemently—

Yes, we have.

ELIAZAR (CHIEF PHARISEE)

Glum—

No one will dare to get into an argument with him again... no chance of winning—and then the fear of losing face in front of the people. But keeping silent will invite greater troubles.

CHIEF PRIEST

Fearful about something happening does not necessarily make it happen.

ELIAZAR (CHIEF PHARISEE)

What benefit have we got by chasing him and his disciples out of the church? Now, he roams the streets and the seashore preaching. Offerings at the temple are dwindling by the day.

ANANYAS (HIGH PRIEST)

Angrily—

Money, money, money. You have nothing else to talk of. No amount of it can satisfy you.

ELIAZAR (CHIEF PHARISEE)

Show me anyone who'll ever say he has had enough.

ANANYAS (HIGH PRIEST)

You're right; the thirst for easy money is unquenchable. You'll find none who would say enough!

PHARISEE

Get ready for people's curses and abuses. They are looking at us with contempt.

ANANYAS (HIGH PRIEST)

Vexed—

We have lowered ourselves in front of them. Pretense won't work anymore. Our actions should match our professions.

With crossed arms, he pauses, thinking.

I see only one way out.

ELIAZAR (CHIEF PHARISEE)

Unless some way is found soon enough, we're altogether lost.

ANANYAS (HIGH PRIEST)

We must somehow persuade the people that he is driving out demons with the help of Beelzebub, their head.

PRIEST

I now recall Phinahas saying a woman was healed by just touching his garment.

ELIAZAR (CHIEF PHARISEE)

So what?

PRIEST

We must spread the news that he is wearing Prophet Elijah's mantle.

The ELIAZAR (CHIEF PHARISEE) and the ANANYAS (HIGH PRIEST) give each other a cunning glance.

PRIEST

A similar news spread not long ago said that John the Baptist was wearing Elijah's garment. It is also believed that the garment Elijah gave to Elisha is preserved in the Jerusalem temple.

ELIAZAR (CHIEF PHARISEE)

Now I get it! Brilliant thinking by Phinahas! Zacharia stole Elijah's garment from the temple, and by its power he got a son at a ripe old age. His son, John the Baptist, donated that garment to his close relative Jesus, who works miracles by its power. Yes! Now we've got a handle on it!

ANANYAS (HIGH PRIEST)

That is what we call practical thinking. Zacharia is a priest who serves in the Jerusalem temple. It was while praying in the temple that he became speechless. Mary, the mother of Jesus, is the niece of Elizabeth, Zacharia's wife. We shall spread the news that they belong to a family that has lunacy in their genes. It can also be alleged that they are doing all this as part of a larger conspiracy.

Laughs—

The people will lap it up.

PRIEST

But what about the raising of Lazarus from the dead? How will we handle it?

ELIAZAR (CHIEF PHARISEE)

Why not kill Lazarus again in the presence of the people and ask Jesus to raise him from the dead once more? That surely won't happen. People can thereafter be easily convinced that Lazarus did not die at all and that the story of him being raised from the dead is dishonest propaganda.

ANANYAS (HIGH PRIEST)

But what if he raises Lazarus from the dead a second time? The people will hail him as the Messiah all the more. We will be hounded by the multitude that throng to him. We and our future generations will thus be stripped of priesthood.

ELIAZAR (CHIEF PHARISEE)

Head lowered, thinking—

Must do something drastic, or things will get out of hand completely. Our and Phinahas will be here any moment. After they come, we must put our heads together and hatch a solution. There is nothing for which they lack a solution.

Then, keep shuffling across the stage.

Lights fade out slowly.

SCENE 8

JESUS and the DISCIPLES are on the stage. Light falls on the front half of the stage. The shadow of a mountain and adjacent village appears on the back curtain.

The light falls on THOMAS DIDYMUS, JOHN, ANDREW, JUDAS, and PETER. The other disciples appear as shadows behind them.

JESUS

I am giving you a piece of advice, which will be for you a new Commandment. The days of Aaron's tribe and its priesthood are numbered. The time has come for the Son of Man to be sacrificed for the salvation of humankind. You'll be cleansed of the stain of sin. The spell of the Original Sin and all other sins will be broken. With the annulment of the bondage of sin, the need for its forgiveness and reparation, too, will become redundant. The priesthood Moses instituted will no longer have any role to play. I give you instead the regal priesthood of Melchizedek. It does not involve burned offerings, purification offerings, or cash offerings. The sacrifice you shall offer is service in love. The priesthood that will be conferred on you by the blood of the Messiah is not of the flesh. It is heavenly and eternal. The days of ritual worship are over. Love one another as children of God. All sacrifices have been rendered meaningless by the supreme sacrifice of the Son of Man. Is there anything that can compensate for the blood of the Son of God? This will be the last and final sacrifice offered to God upon this earth.

PETER

If God detests the worship of idols, why doesn't He destroy them?

JESUS

To efface idolatry from the face of the earth, God will have to destroy the sun and the moon, too, which are worshipped by countless people. It is human nature to seek God somewhere out there but remain willfully blind to the God within.

ANDREW

Won't we have to offer ritual worship to God anymore?

JESUS

The Creator doesn't depend on his creation for sustenance. The Vine doesn't use wine derived from its fruit for its sustenance. Does anyone use olive oil as fertilizer for the olive tree? The Creator has little to do with your worldly notions and enterprises. You're using yourselves, your ways, and your means as the standards to weigh and value God.

JUDAS

Why does God let the righteous suffer?

JESUS

Suppose you have a pair of oxen. One is lame in one foot. The other is the equivalent of some supernatural power. Which of these would you put to the yoke?

JUDAS

The one that has power.

JESUS

The potter selects the best pot by tapping them many times with fingers. Those which sound brittle, he puts aside. God tests the just man, fully knowing that his faith is strong enough to endure.

PETER

Teach us to pray, Master.

JESUS

You must address your prayer to your Father, who is in Heaven. He is the reason for all things that exist and for what they are—the one who scrutinizes your thoughts and feelings. He knows what your needs are even before you ask of Him. Pray with an innocent, loving heart that seeks no favors. Pray, asking for God's grace for serving and loving one another. Caught between the Red Sea and the Egyptians, the people of Israel cried to God for help. God chastised Moses, asking: Why cry? Why pray? The lamentations of my people have reached me long before your prayer. Stretch forward your staff to the sea and see it split apart. For God, none of his creations is smaller or bigger than the other. All of them are equally of great worth. All of them pray to him. When you trust the light within yourself, you're trusting in God, who is in you. If you believe that, then God will surely hear and honor your prayer.

THOMAS

Skeptically—

All the same, it is a fact that God doesn't always hear the prayers of the righteous.

JESUS

The righteous man is a discriminating and divisive idea of your shallow thinking. Who can claim to be righteous in the presence of God?! Can any man claim to be more righteous than Moses? And yet he was so humble before God! Humbler than any other human being.

Nevertheless, God denied him the reward of entering the land of Canaan. You have turned prayer into a tool of coercion and convenience. You pride yourself on your noble births or achievements. Even while you ask and receive what you deserve, you should rely totally on Yahweh with a simple and humble heart. That alone is the proof that you love God. Then the Lord of mercy will hold you dear to his bosom and cover you with His kindness.

Pause

Place your hope more in doing the will of God than in prayer. Find joy in doing so. God will bestow his blessings in abundance on those who take pity on the hungry, the hapless, and the poor. An angel of God is there standing on the right-hand side of the beggar who comes to your door. To those who show mercy to their brethren in distress, the heavenly Father will also show mercy.

If you throw your bread on water, after a considerable amount of time, you'll get it back multi-fold. God uses sinners to create wealth that'll benefit those in whom he is well pleased. The wealth of the rich man, on the other hand, deprives him of sleep. The blessing of the Lord may help wealth to grow. Choose wisdom over wealth. Wisdom is to be treasured above all other riches of this world, as King Solomon did. Wisdom uplifts and illuminates life, but silence is its treasured protection.

SCENE 9

Wielding a whip, JESUS is roaring like a ferocious tiger. Coins, chairs, bird cages, etc., are strewn around. The shadow of the pillars of the Jerusalem temple appears on the back curtain. In the background are heard the shouts and cries of people.

JESUS

Holding the whip aloft—

Woe to you Levitical priests who have turned the house of God into a marketplace! For what you perform here are not holy sacrifices or ritual worship. They are schemes and superstitions devised by you to extort money. The temple, my Father's house, shall be a house of prayer, not a marketplace of priestly covetousness. You have instead turned it into a temple for Mammon, just like the temple tower dedicated to Babel.

PHARISEE

At the top of his voice—

This is God's temple, and we are its custodians. You may want to capture it, but the writ of Herod alone runs here.

JESUS

You set a price even for sparrows and swallows. Who made them? You, or God? You offer them as reparation for your evil deeds. Your priestly reparations for sins must be offered periodically. I am offering you the inheritance of eternal salvation. I have bought the rights of this temple by offering a great price in exchange. This is not the house of God; it is just a marketplace, and you are merchants of priestly goods and services.

PRIEST

You're a loud-mouthed rebel, poorer than a temple mouse.

Pause

Herod doesn't need to sell this temple to build a magnificent palace for himself.

JESUS

I shall now sanctify this temple and perform the dedication of a new type of temple. This ceremony of mine shall be commemorated in every corner of the earth until the end of times. No more temples shall be built. Have you not heard it said that Yahweh does not live in manmade houses? When the people asked prophet Samuel to give them a king, Yahweh dissuaded them, forewarning the dangers it entailed. When they insisted on getting a king, Yahweh gave in to their demand. And see the result! The same is true of the priesthood Yahweh bestowed on Aaron. It has befallen on me as the liberator of the human race to help them to transcend it.

To the disciples—

He who believes in me shall enjoy everlasting peace. You shall all become inheritors of a new priesthood, a royal priesthood of the same heavenly priest, Melchizedek. He was far greater than Aaron. You should share it with everyone who believes in me. All of them have a right to it. It is a priesthood of love. God shall purify you of your sins and build his abode with you and within you. In it, you shall serve and worship him. What pleases Yahweh most is a humble heart. Yahweh is pleased with it. Yahweh dwells in it.

MYSTERIOUS VOICE

Shadow of a cross appears on the back screen and slowly dissolves out.

The kingdom of God. The kingdom of love. The kingdom of God is within you.

SCENE 10

ASHER (ROMAN GENERAL), the ANANYAS (HIGH PRIEST),
and the CENTURION are standing at the dimly lit part of the
stage conversing. The ELIAZAR (CHIEF PHARISEE) rushes in,
panting. His dress is crumpled, and hair disheveled. Looks totally
unkempt. Two panic-stricken PHARISEES rush in after him.

ELIAZAR (CHIEF PHARISEE)

Panting—

Is there no one here? Or has everyone suddenly gone deaf and dumb?
O yes! You sure can't speak when your mouths are stuffed with food,
as always.

ANANYAS (HIGH PRIEST)

It looks like something has come stung you on the way.

CENTURION

Rather, someone has stopped him on his way and rubbed him down.

He rubs down his body.

ASHER (ROMAN GENERAL)

Has anything strange and untoward happened?

ELIAZAR (CHIEF PHARISEE)

Amused—

Strange and untoward is everything that happens these days.

ANANYAS (HIGH PRIEST)

If burglars have got away with the temple collection, let them.

Pause, looking somewhat puzzled.

How can that be? Barabbas and notorious burglars like him are locked up in jail. Who then?

ELIAZAR (CHIEF PHARISEE)

The notorious ones may be locked up, but someone worse is on the rampage; and that too, in the Jerusalem Temple.

ANANYAS (HIGH PRIEST)

Indignant—

None who displays arrogance in the temple of Yahweh will be
spared. Think of it: he thinks he can denigrate God's temple too!

To the general—

What's happening here? Where are your soldiers?

CENTURION

Things are happening just as I expected. I can see only one way out.

He ponders.

ELIAZAR (CHIEF PHARISEE)

Takes out an empty money bag from his pocket and holds it aloft.

There is only one way left to me: destitution. This bag is empty.
Unless it is replenished, my dear soul—

Pause

—pardon me, my stomach, I mean, won't be at peace.

PHARISEE

I lost my money, and my dress got crumpled. I wonder how seriously
people will take me from now on.

CHIEF PRIEST

Gravely to the general—

What is needed now is a thoroughly whetted plan.

ASHER (ROMAN GENERAL)

As far as possible, we must avoid bloodshed. It is important that we ensure the people have a hearty time during the festival. For that, a peaceful environment is necessary.

ELIAZAR (CHIEF PHARISEE)

Yes, we need a peaceful environment to make up for what we have lost.

ANANYAS (HIGH PRIEST)

To the general—

Greed for money is an incurable disease indeed.

CENTURION

The same is true of thirst for power.

He prepares to exit.

Must come to a resolute decision immediately—just for a morale booster.

SCENE 11

The stage is set the same way as before. When the lights come on, the ANANYAS (HIGH PRIEST) is seen crisscrossing the stage, expecting someone to arrive. The ELIAZAR (CHIEF PHARISEE) and two OTHER PHARISEES rush in, panting. They are in a panic, and their clothes are crumpled.

ANANYAS (HIGH PRIEST)

What's the matter with you? Have you gone mad or what? Whatever be the crisis, we will find a solution for it.

ELIAZAR (CHIEF PHARISEE)

You can't find a solution for this. Forty days of fasting, penance, and prayer are but a poor remedy for it.

ANANYAS (HIGH PRIEST)

To the other Pharisees

What is the meaning of all this?

ELIAZAR (CHIEF PHARISEE)

Rend your garments! The echo of an unforgivable sin is ringing in my ears. It presages an unhinged mind.

ANANYAS (HIGH PRIEST)

You're right; he has gone out of his mind.

The ELIAZAR (CHIEF PHARISEE) gestures to the other Pharisees. They exit.

THE ELIAZAR (CHIEF PHARISEE)

Dolefully—

The foundation for this temple was laid by David's son Solomon with the blessings and wealth bestowed on him by Yahweh.

ANANYAS (HIGH PRIEST)

Horrified—

What has befallen the temple? Tell us!

ELIAZAR (CHIEF PHARISEE)

I will be blaspheming with my tongue if I utter it. That Nazarene is boasting... that he will destroy and rebuild it in three days. That is the one redline he shouldn't have crossed. He must be made to pay dearly for it. Yes. He will pay for it mightily. Here, I rend my garment.

ANANYAS (HIGH PRIEST)

He's gone crazy. No doubt about that! Must have been high on drugs. Heady mushrooms are available aplenty now. This is blasphemy. There is nothing worse that you could hear.

Brokenhearted—

Here, I, too, rend my garment—smear ash on my head.

He attempts to rend his garment but fails.

Damn it! Oh, you, insensitive garments! Give way. May burning coal be showered on my God-forsaken head!

Both of them together attempt to rend the garment of the ELIAZAR (CHIEF PHARISEE) by pulling it hard. The force of their efforts makes the ELIAZAR (CHIEF PHARISEE) fall to the ground.

The sound of cloth being torn apart is heard.

ELIAZAR (CHIEF PHARISEE)

The garment has been rent at last! Now, I shall smear ash on my head and fast for forty days.

ANANYAS (HIGH PRIEST)

Looking with squinted eyes—

What is rent? Your rich rob or your stinking undergarment?

SCENE 12

JESUS and THE DISCIPLES sit on one side of the stage. The SENIOR DISCIPLES sit under the light. The rest of the disciples and a small crowd are visible on the back curtain.

JESUS

You're the inheritors of Heaven. The devil entered the heavenly Garden of Eden God created on Earth and cheated man and woman out of it, tempting them with the delusion of worldly glory. He continues his mission of seduction to this day. Wherever paradise is created, the devil sneaks in, in various shapes and ways. He wins peoples' confidence, tempts them with luring offers, and leads them to their perdition. Therefore, be on your guard. Strive for true knowledge. So, be you innocent as doves, cunning as serpents, and keen-sighted as eagles. Take care not to forfeit Heaven for worldly trinkets.

The ANANYAS (HIGH PRIEST), a PRIEST, the ELIAZAR (CHIEF PHARISEE), a PHARISEE, and two other followers enter.

ANANYAS (HIGH PRIEST)

Addressing Jesus—

You, Jesus, we know who you, your parents, and your siblings are. How can you and your disciples then claim that you are the Son of God? On what authority are you spreading this canard?

JESUS

Do you not sing a psalm that says you are gods; you are all sons of the Most High? You don't get it. You don't think; you grope in the dark. Adorning yourself with high titles and gaudy robes, you swagger and jockey for positions of honor and profit. God knows your heart is set not on God but on the coveted seats of honor, here and in Heaven. I have come to prepare for those who believe in my heavenly Father an eternal heavenly abode that no termite or worms will corrupt. There is a chasm between your ways and mine.

PRIEST

You have insulted and belittled our priesthood. We have suffered enough and more humiliation because of you. You have undermined our pride and prestige. The limit is reached. Enough is enough.

ELIAZAR (CHIEF PHARISEE)

You rate the abominable Samaritans, who refuse to obey the Laws and directives of Moses, higher than us.

PRIEST

You and your disciples have become Samaritans. Who are you really, Jews or Samaritans?

JESUS

You have divided the children of God into various tribes and races and color-coded them in parochial and sectarian identities. You deny them entry into the house of God. On what basis you do this? Which race does God belong to? When did God claim to be of a higher race?

PETER

You make slaves even of the Israelites. You consider some as inferior to the rest. To you, the poor are worthless, meant only to be your menial servants. You despise them and treat the orphans callously and the widows lecherously.

ANDREW

Don't you think that God's provisions apply to them too? Don't they also deserve to be set free in the Sabbatical year? The year of liberation?

JESUS

Woe to you, priests! You pretend to be punctilious about your priestly costumes and earnest about the priestly practices handed down to you by Aaron, but you neither care for them nor understand them. The people who began their journey to Canaan from Mizraim were of a mixed race. Many of them had brought disrepute to Jewish beliefs, customs, and traditions by cohabiting with Egyptian women. To lead his people on the right path and to mitigate some of the heavy responsibility Moses was shouldering, God asked him to anoint Aaron as priest. God had set a time limit for this arrangement in His plan. You have instead corrupted and perpetuated it, misusing it as an ungodly means to rob the people and to lord over them. And how hugely you enjoy the profit and pleasures of it! Still not satisfied, you find pleasure in crippling and burdening the people with the guilt of sin. You rob widows of their meager mites and use them to build mansions of pride, sin, and disgrace. You don't even spend a lowly copper coin to bring succor to them. Have you not read in the Scripture that Yahweh values kindness and divine knowledge above rituals and sacrifices? Your deceit and hypocrisy have slammed the doors of Heaven shut against your face. You don't want to enter Heaven, nor will let anyone enter therein either. On Mount Horeb, Yahweh divested Aaron of his priesthood... did not allow him to enter Canaan. How do you then expect Him to allow you into heavenly Canaan? You continue with what you did in Gilgal. Your costumes are gilt with pride, and your face painted with shallowness. You are an abomination to Yahweh.

ANANYAS (HIGH PRIEST)

I find your wild denunciations baseless, bizarre, and weird. They are a scandal and calumny to priesthood. You are nobody to denounce, much less destroy priesthood. Mountains may shake and fall into the sea, but priesthood will remain.

JESUS

Woe to you, priests! You, who are walking in the dark, can only lead others to darkness because you deceive people by hiding behind a façade of hypocrisy. Aaron and his chosen followers conducted worship at the Arc of the Covenant by burning incense and offering sacrifices in the tent of the Lord's presence. When your worship degenerated into idol worship, Yahweh hid the Arc of the Covenant. But you cheat the people, continuing to offer worship in the vacant place behind the cover of a curtain. Your hearts are wicked, and your mind vacuous. Take a peep into, if you dare, and see for yourself.

Pause

Why do you think Yahweh chose to preserve Moses' body? Ever thought about it?

ANDREW

Pointing to the ANANYAS (HIGH PRIEST)—

Or, else you would have built a temple, and expanded your business.

PETER

Don't forget that Satan is still hunting for Moses's body.

PRIEST

Don't we have to offer sacrifices of atonement for the sins of the people? It gives them the much-needed solace. There is nothing else that does.

ANDREW

You profit from their guilt. The greater their sins, the bigger the ransom you require of them as sacrifices of atonement.

JESUS

You are hand in glove with the Roman rulers to oppress and exploit the people, who must do back-breaking work to eke out a living. Over and above the back-breaking taxes imposed by their colonial oppressors, you put on them a heavy load of guilt for the sins you invent to fleece them.

PRIEST

You boast to be a heavenly accredited, incredibly generous forgiver of sins. But how can you, a carpenter, offer something over which God alone has authority to do?

JESUS

You admit that God alone has the power to forgive sins. Then, how come you perform innumerable prayers, rituals, and sacrifices for the remission of sins?

ANANYAS (HIGH PRIEST)

We are only continuing with the sacrifices prescribed according to the Law of Moses, the directions of Aaron, and the dictates of the Jewish tradition. The people can't do without it. If the people have no complaints, then why should you bother?

JESUS

The truth is only God and the Son of Man have the authority to forgive sins. Your sacrifices are of no value. You call your handiwork of bricks and mud the abode of God. By what power do you bring God under your control? By what power do you invoke God to limit his presence to it? Just by dint of the few sentences you chant! What makes you think that God is your slave to be at your beck and call? The God who created this universe is present in its every nook and corner. What better abode is there for him than the hearts of men and women whom he created in his own image? God will raze your work of hands to the ground. Crawling creatures will make its ruins their abode. Certainly, they are of much greater worth in the eyes of God. Know this, the days of your priesthood are numbered.

ELIAZAR (CHIEF PHARISEE)

Arrogance has got into your head. You declare that you are the Son of God and gloat in it. We hold fast to Jewish traditions and the Law of Moses. We will transform the Jewish people into a great nation and thus build up a divine empire. When the Messiah comes, he will reward us adequately. The problem is you; you alone are the problem. It is high time that you minded what has taken possession of you.

JESUS

Woe to you, Pharisees, for you aid and abet priests in assisting the Roman rulers in suppressing the people. You have shredded the Ten Commandments of Moses into one thousand and sixty-five bits. You use each of them to make money. You've appropriated for a price the right to determine that there is no leaven in unleavened bread or if the sacrificial lamb has any blemish. You are partakers of a system that is exploiting and degrading the people. You'll pay a heavy price for it. Sadly, you have dragged your progeny too into it.

PHARISEE

Enraged—

You are denigrating all who are engaged in God's work. If you're indeed a prophet, reveal where the Arc of the Covenant can be found.

JESUS

Aggrieved by your trespasses, Yahweh has handed it over to the Philistines. When you turned it into a token of idol worship and a means to amass wealth, Yahweh quietly hid it from you. It has crossed the sea in a ship. The ship that carried it suffered the same miserable fate as the Philistines. Keep on searching till you find it.

Pause

The Messiah will recover it at his second coming. Your children will prophesy. They will turn against you. They will thrash your trickery under their feet. Your days, too, are counted.

ANANYAS (HIGH PRIEST)

To the ELIAZAR (CHIEF PHARISEE)—

He will never walk the right path. I gave him one last chance, which has proved a waste of time. The time has come for us to decide what is to be done with him. It is time to think of the final solution.

They all exit.

JESUS

Watches those who are exiting—

I shall reduce the laws and Commandments of Moses into just two precepts for you. Firstly, adore the Lord your God with all your soul, all your heart, all your mind, and all your body. Secondly, love your neighbor, whom also the Lord has created in His own image, as yourself. These two commandments contain all the rest. Love is the essence of God. It is the light of life and the sustaining force of all creation.

Pause

If only you strictly adhere to the Commandment to love one another, you will gain favor with God. You are my disciples only if you love one another. Take this message of love and liberation to the ends of the earth. This is the sole mission that I am giving you.

MYSTERIOUS VOICE

Love of God, love of neighbor, love of God, love of God—love—the world—creation through love—creation—

Peters down as an echo.

End of Act II

A short break— Loud music.

ACT III | SCENE I

The stage is dimly lit. JESUS' riding on a donkey appears as shadow on the back curtain. People shouting "Hosanna! Hosanna to the Son of God!" reverberates. On the curtain, people waving palm leaves are seen scampering. Light falls on the front half of the stage. Standing there are THOMAS, ANDREW, JOHN, and JUDAS.

THOMAS

Pointing out to the donkey—

Does this donkey speak?

ANDREW

You think it is the direct descendant of Balaam's donkey, or what?

JUDAS

The one who is riding it now is not someone who will curse Israel for money. As the heir of King David, he is reviving the remembrance of what his great ancestor did. He is following the traditions set by King David and King Solomon.

JOHN

On the back of this donkey now begins the journey of the world's redemption. That animal is a symbol of everlasting peace.

ANDREW

The liberation of people from the decadent priesthood is at hand, and this opens the door to a new vision for humanity.

JUDAS

The prophecy of Zacharia is being fulfilled here and now. This is the day of liberation for the temple from decadent priesthood and of Israel from the Romans.

THOMAS

Wielding his sword, an angel of God stopped Balaam from proceeding to the Jerusalem Temple. His donkey saw the angel blocking the way and refused to move. Balaam beat the donkey thrice. God told Balak that He won't speak falsehood like men. Indeed, the Son of God, the truth incarnates, is traveling to the Jerusalem Temple, which of late has become, alas, a symbol of iniquity.

ANDREW

The time has arrived for the fulfillment of Isaiah's prophesy. A day will come when the children of Israel will bring offerings on donkey's back to the Jerusalem Temple. The lamb to be sacrificed to atone for the sins of the people is riding on a donkey to the temple— a sacrificial lamb by his own choice.

The light fades out.

SCENE 2

JESUS is seated at the dining table—also, PETER, ANDREW, JUDAS, THOMAS DIDYMUS, and JOHN. The rest of the disciples are seen as shadows. JESUS breaks bread into pieces and gives them to the disciples. He pours out a drink from a vessel for the disciples.

JESUS

This house has now received peace and tranquility. The scorn that was attached to Matthew's name has disappeared.

Pause

The Christ has come to save sinners, the destitute, and the tax collectors. The Son of Man brings justice to those who thirst for it.

MARY MAGDALENE enters cautiously. Her hair is flowing loosely. The expression on her face is one of radiant gratitude flavored with contrition. She is holding an alabaster jar of costly

perfume. JESUS turns toward her. The disciples are taken aback.
She slowly walks up to JESUS and sits at his feet.

PETER

To the others in a whisper—

There she is once again. What does she mean?

MARY anoints JESUS's feet with the perfume. Kisses them. Dries them
with her hair. When the scent of the perfume fills the room, the disciples
look at each other in incomprehension.

JUDAS

In a whisper to Peter—

It is an extremely costly perfume—top-notch. The money paid for it
could have been put to better use. Sheer avoidable waste. It had
better be given to the poor.

PETER

She must be showing her gratitude to Jesus for driving out demons
from her. Showing gratitude is praiseworthy, except that she defiles
Jesus by touching him. Impertinent woman!

JESUS

To Peter—

She had been sorely distressed by evil spirits. But now she is healed
and restored.

ANDREW

But the people say she is deranged.

THOMAS

It's true she suffers from fits. Because she rolled on the ground and thrashed about, people concluded that she was possessed.

Pause

She was deemed weird and shunned by all.

JUDAS

A daughter's incurable disease has brought indelible shame to the family of Magdala's headman.

PETER

Indignantly—

What right does she have to walk into a room where we are? And that, too, on an occasion like this?

JESUS

What are you grumbling about, Peter? Has not the scent of this perfume cleansed and renewed you? Has it not refreshed your soul.? If you still despise this woman, how are you different from the insensitive people around her?

Turning to Mary—

Woman, this act of yours has a meaning that you are now not fully aware. But it will soon come to light. It anticipates and honors my death. You have washed and kissed my feet, rubbing perfume on them. Preserve this perfume for the day when you rub me with it head to foot to give me the final farewell.

Turning to Peter—

Peter, can't you see God's image in her? Aren't women and men alike the creations of God? Why do you then look down upon her? She is as dear to me as you, my disciple.

PETER looks at the other disciples in disbelief.

JUDAS

How on Earth can we consider this fallen woman like one of us!?

JESUS

Time will open your eyes, and then you will know she is a true disciple. Only then will your eyes be opened.

ANDREW

He is following the footsteps of Joshua.

Sighing—

That part of the Scripture, too, must be fulfilled thus.

The lights fade out.

SCENE 3

When light returns, JESUS is seen sitting at one side of the table.
PETER, JUDAS, THOMAS DIDYMUS, ANDREW, and JOHN are
also there on the stage. The other apostles are visible as shadows on
the back curtain.

JESUS

I have chosen you as shepherds of the people of Israel. You're also the
preachers of a new teaching. I am sending you as sheep among
wolves. Those who follow my footsteps will have to suffer for it.
Those who refuse to carry the cross cannot follow me and be my
disciples.

JESUS asks the disciples to sit around the table. Only those who
are on the stage are visible. The others appear just as shadows.
JESUS wraps a towel around his waist and begins to wash the feet
of the disciples, from right to left, starting with John. He reaches
Andrew and Peter last.

JESUS

I consider you as my brothers. You, too, should be so to each other.
There should be neither master nor slave among you. You are all of
one body and one soul in me. All are equal. Where there is love,
equality prevails. You should not covet or seek any position of
worldly distinction or honor. You should not prefer to be called Rabi
or Father. Yahweh alone is your Father, as well as the Father of all
human beings. To desire to be called Father is like claiming equality
with God is tantamount to taking God's name in vain. You should
not desire to be called Rabi or Master. God alone is the source of all
wisdom. He alone can reveal the ultimate truth to you. Who in the
world is wiser than Solomon? Don't you know how he acquired his
wisdom?

JESUS begins to wash PETER's feet.

PETER

I am not worthy to be touched by your divine hands, Master. Allow
me to wash and kiss your feet.

JESUS

Let your journey to Heaven start here, Peter. You are beginning a new
journey in the new way I revealed to you. I am washing your feet not
into physical cleanliness but into spiritual beauty. Feet expresses the
beauty of the soul better than the face. The new journey needs new
feet, Peter. Beware, lest you are led astray by worldly cares.

Pause

The historical journey these feet must make is just getting started.

PETER

Excited—

If so, wash me, head to foot, Master.

JESUS

Peter, you know not what you say; I am preparing your feet for a new way, a new journey. If the feet are clean, then the whole body is clean.

To the disciples as a whole—

Do this in remembrance of me. Love one another and serve one another as I have loved you. Only then will peace reign amongst you. Only by that will you be known as my disciples. You are the keepers of Heaven's keys. You'll make a paradise of this earth. The spirit of truth and love will guide you in this divine mission. Stay true to this calling, and you will come to be known as my disciples. Take my teaching to heart. My journey is coming to an end, and yours must begin now.

The light fades out.

SCENE 4

The ELIAZAR (CHIEF PHARISEE) and the PRIEST ELIHU are on the stage with arms crossed over their chests, daring and expectant. They are expecting someone. They look in the direction of the entrance door now and again. The ANANYAS (HIGH PRIEST) and the CENTURION enter.

ELIAZAR (CHIEF PHARISEE)

Dismayed—

Amazing! Incredible! How could it have happened?!

PRIEST

It is like sneaking into the king's palace and winning over his minister.

TWO PHARISEES rush in, panting and in panic.

PHARISEE

What! Did I hear it right?

ANANYAS (HIGH PRIEST)

Hold your horses. We will soon know if it is clinched.

He looks in the direction of the opposite door.

PRIEST

Utterly incredible! How did you clinch it?

ANANYAS (HIGH PRIEST)

Laughing heartily—

There is one thing that no one can resist—you have it a bit more than others—money. Is there anyone who wouldn't fall for it? Remember, even prophets have been bought in the past!

PRIEST

I had little hope it would work.

ANANYAS (HIGH PRIEST)

To the centurion—

Here, again, is proof of his brilliant thinking and flawless execution, unmatchable indeed!

CENTURION

I weighed the information gathered by our spies and concluded that they were worth a gamble. Wait until we know for sure I have hit the bull's eye.

ELIAZAR (CHIEF PHARISEE)

He is no easy prey, and therefore, my anxiety... I know his father and his father's younger brother quite well. Accursed is his whole family!

PHARISEE

His father, Simeon, and his uncle, Mileah, are famous people.

ELIAZAR (CHIEF PHARISEE)

Yes, yes, they are Pharisees. His father is a well-known interpreter of dreams. His uncle does fortune-telling using Hebrew letters and numbers. It has made him very rich indeed.

PRIEST

That makes things a little clearer. They revived Gematria, a forgotten fortune-telling method. They developed it into a highly profitable enterprise. Its fame spread all over Israel and abroad. Soon, they became stinking rich.

PRIEST

Then suddenly, they shut shop...

Thinking

—as if something untoward had happened.

ELIAZAR (CHIEF PHARISEE)

So cruel was his son's betrayal that it incapacitated him altogether.

PRIEST

Incredulously—

What happened?

ELIAZAR (CHIEF PHARISEE)

A leading Pharisee family coming to grief! Thanks to a delinquent son?

CENTURION

But the son didn't lead a wayward life, did he?

ANANYAS (HIGH PRIEST) *Looks incredulously at the centurion.*

CENTURION

Spying is our job, and we're rather good at it. The promising son, the family pride, leaves home and goes to the desert to become a monk.

ELIAZAR (CHIEF PHARISEE)

You're right; he joined the Essenes. Thus he...

CENTURION

He became a companion of the Essene, John. Became his thick friend. It was he who provided food and water to John in the desert.

ANANYAS (HIGH PRIEST)

Which means he's no small fry. He's much more than what we consider him to be.

ELIAZAR (CHIEF PHARISEE)

Is it true that he visited John in the prison?

CENTURION

Yes, he did.

A SOLDIER suddenly enters.

SOLDIER

The man you were expecting is here.

CENTURION

Send him in.

The SOLDIER exits.

JUDAS enters. Everyone looks at him anxiously. JUDAS surveys each of them.

CENTURION

We were eagerly awaiting you.

ANANYAS (HIGH PRIEST)

Have no doubt all of us are of one mind. None will come to know what takes place here.

PRIEST

There's nothing special happening here after all. We just wanted to see a trusted disciple of Jesus. We sent for you, and you obliged, that's all.

ANANYAS (HIGH PRIEST)

We were just speaking about your renowned father and uncle.

PRIEST

How can you, of all people, tolerate the company of tax collectors and fishermen?

ELIAZAR (CHIEF PHARISEE)

If you help us in a small thing we have in mind, you'll get a chance to rejoin us. Even if you don't go back to your father's profession, you still can find other ways to earn lots of money.

JUDAS flashes a look of suspicion.

ANANYAS (HIGH PRIEST)

Judas, you alone can help us. It is hardly possible to identify this man Jesus from his disciples in daylight, let alone at night.

ELIAZAR (CHIEF PHARISEE)

He and that Thomas Didymus are so much alike in their looks and deportment that only when he opens his mouth can you recognize that he is Jesus of Nazareth.

PRIEST

Since he is always surrounded by people during the day, sending the soldiers to arrest him then could trigger bloodshed. It is foolish to risk bloodshed, especially when it can be avoided.

ANANYAS (HIGH PRIEST)

This, indeed, is a trivial matter. Come with us to meet Caiaphas in his palace. His wife would like to meet Jesus in person—maybe to be cured of some disease. You know it is awkward for her to go to him.

CENTURION

Just meet him and answer a question or two he may have. I assure you this is no more than a formality. He could also take comfort in his wife's wish being fulfilled. Along with you, we also can derive comfort from having done a good deed. Caiaphas' favor means a lot to us.

ANANYAS (HIGH PRIEST)

Do us this one little favor: help us to identify Jesus from his disciples.

ELIAZAR (CHIEF PHARISEE)

Takes out a pair of scissors from his pocket.

Here, take this. Just trim the hair and beard of Thomas Didymus with it. We will then be able to pick Jesus on our own.

CENTURION

You stand to lose nothing by doing so.

ANANYAS (HIGH PRIEST)

There's nothing in it that can cause you harm or loss. Furthermore, you get a chance to make a fortune.

ELIAZAR (CHIEF PHARISEE)

Takes out a silver coin from his pocket.

Ask as many as you want of this, and we will give them to you, enough even to buy an ample vineyard.

The ANANYAS (HIGH PRIEST) takes a bulging money bag from his pocket and offers it to JUDAS.

ANANYAS (HIGH PRIEST)

There are thirty silver coins in it. Take it as an advance payment. You will get the big fat balance when the job is done.

CENTURION

Our agents will tell you on which night you are to accomplish it. Give Jesus a kiss. By that, we shall know him.

JUDAS snatches the money bag and exits hurriedly, looking agitated.

ELIAZAR (CHIEF PHARISEE)

What a huge price for a kiss! Those thirty pieces of silver would have sufficed to pay the advance money to buy the best vineyard in the land. Still, you have achieved the impossible with it. Tell me, whose hand should I kiss?

ANANYAS (HIGH PRIEST)

Kiss this centurion's hand if you will, but I don't think it will serve any purpose. Not a coin shall you get.

PRIEST

We will get our rewards from Caiaphas and Pilate.

ELIAZAR (CHIEF PHARISEE)

The very thought of it makes me feel exhilarated. Blessed be the Lord who has made such a thing possible!

ANANYAS (HIGH PRIEST)

To the centurion—

Drag him to Caiaphas as soon as you get hold of him. Not even a hair of him should escape our clutch. Victory is ours.

CENTURION

We will deploy enough soldiers to ensure that none comes between him and us.

ANANYAS (HIGH PRIEST)

I have taken Chief Priest Caiaphas into confidence on this scheme. But there is somebody we have kept as a close secret—Barabbas.

CENTURION

Let it remain so for the time being. The people will be satisfied if someone else is crucified in his place.

ELIAZAR (CHIEF PHARISEE)

Who? Barabbas? But isn't he also a dreaded criminal, a man of violence?

ANANYAS (HIGH PRIEST)

We will only use him as the last resort if all other options fail.

CENTURION

Once we succeed in inciting the people to agitate, the authorities will have to give in to their demands. I have ordered over a hundred soldiers and their assistants to mingle with the people in civil dress. Pilate cannot turn a deaf ear to the clamor of a hundred people. Make no doubt about it. If one plan fails, we'll play the next and the next, and so on, till we succeed.

Stroking down his beard—

My only fear is that Iscariot may deceive us.

PRIEST

Iscariot? Who is that?

CENTURION

The one who left us just now. I don't fully trust him because he keeps jumping from one group to another. He is the disciple of a great radical leader called Iscariot. He is a radical. He is a zealot with quite a history of insurrection. He vowed to bring an end to the Roman occupation by the power of the sword. It was after meeting John in prison that Judas became a disciple of Jesus.

ELIAZAR (CHIEF PHARISEE)

John must have advised him to join this movement. Given that, I find it hard to believe that they trusted him with money matters, especially when there is a well-known tax collector among them who could have done that job far more efficiently.

PRIEST

You think he will take us for a ride? His behavior and bad reputation
give me the hunch that it could prove risky to trust him. Well, well...
let that be. The all-important question is: Will he do so terrible a
thing just for the sake of money?

CENTURION

As a rule, thinkers and dreamers are pathetic when it comes to
practical thinking. His real aim might be something else. We should
be getting a hint of it as we proceed with our plan.

All exit.

MYSTERIOUS VOICE

Thirty silver coins... Thirty silver coins... From Eden to the vineyards
and to the markets of this world, the tinkling, tinkling of gold, silver,
and copper coins.

SCENE 5

The image of Olive Mount falls on the back curtain. JUDAS leisurely enters through a side door. JESUS and the DISCIPLES are standing at the front of the stage. JESUS, ANDREW, PETER, and THOMAS DIDYMUS alone are visible in the dim light. The OTHER DISCIPLES are seated on one side of the stage. As JUDAS enters, the ANANYAS (HIGH PRIEST), ELIAZAR (CHIEF PHARISEE), CENTURION, and a few SOLDIERS appear backstage as shadows.

JUDAS

Ambles in straining to look natural.

Good evening, master!

He goes and kisses JESUS.

JESUS

Judas, how smartly you do what you are assigned to do! This kiss, is it your kiss? And is this your last?

JUDAS turns pale and discomposed. The ELIAZAR (CHIEF PHARISEE), the ANANYAS (HIGH PRIEST), CENTURION, and TWO SOLDIERS rush in. SOLDIERS cluster around as shadows on the back curtain—a bedlam. The SOLDIERS seize JESUS.

ANANYAS (HIGH PRIEST)

Come with us, Jesus of Nazareth. You have disobeyed the Laws of Moses, deprecated the Jewish race, and cast aspersions on the priestly class and the temple. Now off to the High Priest.

Shellshocked, the DISCIPLES look at each other. Pushing back the others, PETER lunges forward.

ELIAZAR (CHIEF PHARISEE)

There is no way for you to escape.

PETER comes forward and stands in front of JESUS.

PETER

To the ANANYAS (HIGH PRIEST)—

Wretch! Despicable wretch! Was it with this in mind that you once put the master to test with questions? You succeeded in turning Judas into a traitor. You have done an accursed thing that will remain a stain on your name and soul forever.

PETER lunges forward and strikes the CENTURION with the sword he snatches from the latter's sheath. As the CENTURION dodges the blow, the sword strikes his cap, making a swishing sound, and slices off his earlobe.

PETER

Keep off you, fiends! What made you think I'll let you take away my master?

JESUS steps forward.

JESUS

Rebukingly—

Oh, Simon, how can you be Cephas and still be carried away like this? See how quickly your rock-solid faith has melted like snow under the sun. Even if you had faith as small as a mustard seed, you wouldn't have acted this way.

He takes away the sword from PETER.

The gains of a sword are illusory, and the kingdom you capture by the sword will fall to other swords. My throne is not of this world; it is of Heaven. It is spiritual. Only that is everlasting. Put the sword back into its sheath. He who wields it will fall by it.

JESUS takes the sword from PETER and hands it over to the centurion.

This sword is drenched in the blood of innocent children. Let your blood be the last that this sword will seek. Blood will always be repaid with blood. I beg pardon of you for the impetuous behavior of my disciple. Love is my message. I have come to serve, not to be served.

He picks up the severed ear of the centurion from the ground and fixes it back on him.

This earlobe should, from now on, resonate with the songs of love.

To all—

Do you really have to come to me in the night to ambush me as though I am a thief or a dangerous lawbreaker? I have come as a messenger of love, and I go happily with you—sheath your swords. Let us go.

To Peter—

Peter, do not waver in your faith. You should now on wield the sword of the Spirit. It is as effective as the fiery sword of the angels. Whatever you gain through the fulfillment of your desires and delusional aspirations won't last long. The kingdoms of this world are made and unmade with the sword of flesh. Their days are numbered. The kingdom of Spirit alone endures.

PETER kneels and covers his face with his hands.

JESUS

Tapping PETER on his shoulder—

Arise. My hour has come. The time is now for the Son of Man to offer his blood as ransom for the world. The Scripture must be fulfilled.

PETER

Sorrowing—

Rabbi, I'm willing to die for your sake. How do you expect me to stand aside and watch these cruel men laying their hands on you?

JESUS

Simon, you're speaking like a man of the world. Fear has gripped your soul. You never have to fear as long as you are with me. Beware of the fear of life; it is the ultimate weapon of this world. Overcome fear, or else you will betray me three times before the dawn breaks.

He puts his hand on PETER's staff.

Let this staff guide you. The sword doesn't suit these soft hands. It will harden the hearts of those who carry it. They'll be ruled by it. They'll shed blood. They'll become a curse on humanity. When swords are beaten into plowshares and sickles, then peace and justice will reign on Earth. Then, shall men reap in joy, bountiful harvests of righteousness.

JESUS moves ahead. Others follow behind. PETER and the OTHER DISCIPLES stand still, benumbed.

Light fades out.

A MYSTERIOUS VOICE

Put the sword in its sheath. Let the sword remain in its sheath. Those who need me will look for me. Those who look for me will find me.

The light fades out into total darkness.

SCENE 6

When the lights come on, the ANANYAS (HIGH PRIEST) is seen sitting at a table with a scroll opened in front of him. Lost in thought, he writes something on it.

The ELIAZAR (CHIEF PHARISEE), ELIHU, and A PHARISEE enter.

ELIAZAR (CHIEF PHARISEE)

Our calculations haven't gone wrong until now. Everything is going according to plan.

ANANYAS (HIGH PRIEST) *turns back to look at him and then continues writing.*

ELIAZAR (CHIEF PHARISEE)

What are you so immersed in writing? Accounts?

ANANYAS (HIGH PRIEST)

Derisively—

Money! Money! Money! Is there nothing else you can think of? I was adding one more name to this list in the scroll. It is the list of those who claimed to be the Messiah and ended up at the gallows. I have added Jesus of Nazareth's name in history books to the list of those delusional saviors and tragic liberators.

JUDAS enters. He becomes everyone's focus of attention. The ELIAZAR (CHIEF PHARISEE) nods to the ANANYAS (HIGH PRIEST). JUDAS reckons everyone.

PHARISEE

We were expecting you, Judas.

ANANYAS (HIGH PRIEST)

Yes, yes. You did us a yeoman service.

ELIAZAR (CHIEF PHARISEE)

Have you paid the advance for the vineyard?

PRIEST

We were just discussing the rest of the money we owe you. You helped us get rid of a terrible worry, and that, too, without involving any bloodshed. It is our desire that you purchase the best vineyard, settle down, and be happy.

ELIAZAR (CHIEF PHARISEE)

Buoyant—

You came to our rescue and in due time. We can never reward you enough.

JUDAS

I don't want your money.

Pause

Tell me, why did you use a despicable criminal like Barabbas as a substitute for Jesus and free him?

ANANYAS (HIGH PRIEST)

Derisively—

Were you expecting us to let him go free after putting him on trial?

ELIAZAR (CHIEF PHARISEE)

The one whom we set free is indeed Bar-Abba, the Son of God.

PHARISEE

Your calculations have misfired.

JUDAS

Now I see. Barabbas is the man after your heart. He suits your character as well. Knowing fully well that he is a robber, a brigand,

and a housebreaker, you liberate him. Could you not instead have set free Simon Ben Gamaliel, whom you fraudulently got jailed?

PRIEST

He is a disciple of John. If we set him free, he will be proclaimed the next Messiah. We will have to start from scratch all over again.

ANANYAS (HIGH PRIEST)

As long as he remains in jail, his speeches will not be heard beyond its unlit walls. You can take comfort in the fact that we have not asked him to be beheaded.

ELIAZAR (CHIEF PHARISEE)

Yet another Messiah? No, please! We don't want to be condemned to starvation.

PHARISEE

I have to feed eight to ten mouths. That's no easy job.

PRIEST

You can take comfort in thinking that you have done the right thing. Thankfully, you came to realize at last that the man you accepted as your teacher and master was not the Messiah.

ELIAZAR (CHIEF PHARISEE)

Weren't all the miracles that made him so popular all fake?

PRIEST

If he did truly possess the divine power he claimed, he would have saved himself.

PHARISEE

I sat awake the whole night in vain, waiting for him work a miracle.

JUDAS

You have not understood him. What greater sacrifice can a man make than giving his own life for the sake of others? He is truly the Son of the Heavenly Father, Bar-Abba—Joshua Ben YHWH—God's own son.

ELIAZAR (CHIEF PHARISEE)

My ears are sore with this blasphemy.

ANANYAS (HIGH PRIEST)

It looks like you have lost your mind. The man you followed is not the Messiah. If indeed he was the Son of God, as you claim, will God allow his son to be crucified?

ELIAZAR (CHIEF PHARISEE)

I understand you have come to get the balance amount. How much is it?

JUDAS

You get me wrong. No, I haven't come for money. You're wrong if you think that I did it for the sake of money. I could have amassed as much money as I wished if cared to. The money that those who were miraculously healed would have given us was limitless. But the master would not agree to accepting a lepton. The gifts received freely from God should freely benefit those in need, he insisted. They should not be used to amass wealth.

PRIEST

Baffled—

For then, why did you do what you have?

JUDAS

My father owns many vineyards. Do I then need your thirty silver coins? It is the price you put on a slave's life—the price you set for the life of the Son of Man.

He takes out a moneybag from his pocket.

Here it is, the money you gave me—all of it—the thirty silver coins you paid as blood money for the sacrificial lamb of God. The Scripture must be fulfilled. It will be.

ELIAZAR (CHIEF PHARISEE)

Puzzled—

Why, then, having known all this, did you choose to betray him?

JUDAS

Staring indignantly—

You still don't know why? I told you the scriptures had to be fulfilled. He came to be a sacrificial lamb for the redemption of mankind. I just happened to be instrumental in it.

ANANYAS (HIGH PRIEST)

You may be upset because things didn't go according to your plan, but that does not justify this silly talk and the gall you display.

PHARISEE

Contrition has put you out of balance.

JUDAS

By crucifying him, you thought you achieved your end. With that, you thought you had got him out of your way once and for all.

ANANYAS (HIGH PRIEST)

Baffled—

As far as we are concerned, he's just a number on the long list of the crucified. He will not have a place in history, even as a footnote.

JUDAS

Scornfully—

You think you are the lords of history? The Truth is not in you. Insecurity plagues you. Greed for power has made you arrogant and irrational.

ELIAZAR (CHIEF PHARISEE)

History is made by the victorious. God is on the side of the victorious.

ANANYAS (HIGH PRIEST)

The name of a Nazarene has been added to the list of the thousands who ended upon the cross.

JUDAS

Scornfully—

You will be witnesses to his victorious return. Have no doubt about it.

ELIAZAR (CHIEF PHARISEE)

Sarcastically—

As the king of taxpayers and sinners? How arrogantly you talk! Over and above betraying your master, you also forget that you sold him for thirty silver coins. Bear the truth.

JUDAS

You will one day witness the appearance of Jesus of Nazareth on the pages of history in bold letters.

ANANYAS (HIGH PRIEST)

Furious—

Along with that will also appear the name of Judas Iscariot, the arch-betrayer who sold his master for a few pieces of silver. With a guilty conscience, you will never find peace nor comfort.

ELIAZAR (CHIEF PHARISEE)

How I wish you had stuck to your father's profession. You would have then known beforehand who this Nazarene was and what fate awaited him. Also, you wouldn't have had to spend the rest of your life self-lacerating, wallowing in soul-corroding guilt and remorse.

JUDAS

Laughing like one unhinged—

I have no regrets. The curse will slither in my soul if I keep the blood money. It is ransom money paid as the price of slavery's shackles.

ELIAZAR (CHIEF PHARISEE)

Whatever you may say, returning the money will not absolve you of the crime of betraying your master. You alone deserve the money. Hell is what you deserve.

JUDAS

I won't hand over this blood money you paid to keep me a slave back to your sinful arms. Let it go back to where it truly belongs – this sacred earth. For the generations to come, the earth will bear witness to your perfidious villainy and your children the sin of calumny.

He throws down the money bag, shattering the coins, and storms out.

ANANYAS (HIGH PRIEST)

Furious—

What impertinence! We shall teach him a lesson or two. We shall lay a trap from which he will never escape.

The ELIAZAR (CHIEF PHARISEE), THE PHARISEE, and the PRIEST gather the scattered coins.

ANANYAS (HIGH PRIEST)

Thinking—

Yes, we must teach him a lesson—a lesson he will never forget.

PHARISEE

Lesson? What kind of a lesson?

ANANYAS (HIGH PRIEST)

With this money, we will purchase the potter's field, which we had meant to. We shall bury the body of this Nazarene in that *Hakeldama*

— field of blood. We shall then make it known to the people that Judas returned the thirty pieces of silver he was paid and that we buried his master in the field we bought with it.

PRIEST

Laughing—

Which is to say, he was buried along with the criminals in whose company he died. The people will find that appropriate and appealing.

ANANYAS (HIGH PRIEST)

This arrogant aleck Judas will thus be remembered in history as the arch-betrayer, the icon of betrayers.

ELIAZAR (CHIEF PHARISEE)

But since he has returned the money, we can't accuse him of greed. Think of it: will anyone in his right senses refuse the money offered to him for the miraculous cure of diseases? Judas could have amassed a fortune that way.

PRIEST

The name of Judas Maccabee will also be tainted because of him. What a pity!

ELIAZAR (CHIEF PHARISEE)

How can we forget that it was Maccabee who aroused the hopes of despairing Israel? This guy, too, owes his name to the clan of Maccabee.

ANANYAS (HIGH PRIEST)

Herod the Great resorted to extreme cruelty to quell that insurgency. The sordid episode has since then remained hanging like a sword over the temple and our priesthood.

PRIEST

You're right; what a huge effort we had to make to maintain priesthood with the dignity and authority it needs! When things were going smoothly, and normalcy returned, there came this fake Messiah. Now that we have thwarted his plan, we can rest in peace and go about our work with our heads held high.

ELIAZAR (CHIEF PHARISEE)

You couldn't have put it better. Besides safeguarding our reputation, we have created for ourselves better prospects for prospering. By God's grace, we have fended off a financial disaster.

ANANYAS (HIGH PRIEST)

So, we're going ahead with buying the potter's field. Get going with the paperwork for it right away. Now begins a new chapter of priesthood with the burial of a fake Messiah in Hakeldama. His reckless misadventure will soon be history.

PRIEST

If only we could bury Judas along with him!

ELIAZAR (CHIEF PHARISEE)

Judas will be a byword of shame and infamy. Not even a puppy will be given the name Judas henceforth.

All burst out in laughter and exit. Light goes out.

SCENE 7

When the curtain rises, the stage is dark. When light comes on, A PHARISEE and a SOLDIER are seen huddled together by the fire. With his face covered, PETER is asleep at the dark end of the stage. People come and go across the stage.

JOHN enters. His head is covered, except for his face.

SOLDIER

I had feared this year's Passover would be an insipid celebration. On the positive side, one more fake Messiah has fallen into our net. On the negative side, a notorious thief has been let loose.

Pausing to think—

I don't think it was right to set Barabbas free for whatever reason. What all terrible crimes he has committed! If you look at it impartially, the Nazarene was a better person. It is hard to believe that he deserved to die. I am afraid it is a terrible miscarriage of justice.

PHARISEE

It doesn't matter much if a thief escapes; he only steals our money and property. Fake Messiahs', on the other hand, steal our hearts and pervert souls. If we had allowed him to live longer, he would have captured the empire itself.

Voice quivering—

That would have denied us our daily bread.

SOLDIER

Where is justice in all this? Truth has been crucified; isn't that what happened, really?

Light falls on PETER. A smile appears on his face. He raises his head, peeps out, and then shouts out—

PETER

I will not eat anything forbidden. I won't even touch it.

He goes back to sleep.

He again awakes with a jolt and shouts out—

Nobody is aware of anything. So, too, am I.

SOLDIER

Whispering to the Pharisee—

He looks like one of the disciples of the Nazarene.

Their eyes engage in consultation. The SOLDIER quietly draws out his sword and pokes PETER with it. PETER pushes it away in sleep. The SOLDIER pokes him again. PETER wakes up, startled, and stares at the sword.

PETER

Agitated—

A sword! a two-edged sword! Take it away. It is smeared with the blood of babies. The sword sullied with the blood of the innocents. Put it back in the sheath. The sword— Innocent babies—

He dozes off again.

PHARISEE

Has everyone gone mad?

The PHARISEE and the SOLDIERS move to a side of the stage.

When PETER wakes again, he sees JOHN sitting beside him, his head covered, revealing only the face.

PETER

Waking again—

I do not know...

Looks at John suspiciously.

JOHN

Come on, complete it, and say I don't know Him.

PETER

What! You, John?

JOHN

Yes, It's I, John. What the master prophesied has happened. You have denied him thrice. Yes, three times!

PETER

When did you regain your speech?

Grieving—

Did I deny the master thrice?

JOHN

You denied the master for fear of life. Take care not to lose your soul, even if you have to lose your life for it.

Covering his head fully, he gets up and walks away.

PETER

Where're you going?

JOHN

I don't fear for my life anymore. I am going to the master. I am walking toward his cross.

He starts walking.

That is all that matters to me.

PETER watches; JOHN exits slowly and deliberately. Light fades out.

SCENE 8

When light comes on again, on the stage are the ANANYAS (HIGH PRIEST), the ARMY COMMANDER, ELIHU, the ELIAZAR (CHIEF PHARISEE), and TWO OTHER PHARISEES.

ELIAZAR (CHIEF PHARISEE)

Things are moving to plan. We can expect a happy ending.

The ANANYAS (HIGH PRIEST) turns to the commander.

COMMANDER

We may have to modify the plan a little.

The ANANYAS (HIGH PRIEST) looks out. A SOLDIER enters, holding a crumbled rob.

SOLDIER

Offering the robe to the ANANYAS (HIGH PRIEST)

The centurion sends this to you.

*Everyone looks at each other in dismay. They approach the soldier
and touch the robe to have a feel of it.*

COMMANDER

Is this not the robe of the Nazarene just crucified?

SOLDIER

Yes, it is. As ordered by the centurion, instead of dividing it amongst
us, we cast lots for it, and the lot fell to me.

*The ANANYAS (HIGH PRIEST) comes forward and takes the robe
from the SOLDIER, who immediately exists.*

ANANYAS (HIGH PRIEST)

This is where the cunningness of Phinehas has saved the day for us.
If it had fallen into the hands of his disciples, they would have used it
to work miracles in his name and made the Nazarene a formidable
Messiah, a greater menace in death than in life

ELIAZAR (CHIEF PHARISEE)

It is in our custody. We can make money by working miracles with it.
I am quite convinced it is Elijah's robe.

PRIEST

We must first try its efficacy by testing it on some sick people. If its power is proven, then an avalanche of affluence awaits us.

PHARISEE

Derisively—

There's no need for all that. The power is not in the cloth but in the superstitious faith of the people. With the slightest effort, people can be made to believe that any rag has miraculous power. Thus, superstitions get converted into super incomes.

ELIAZAR (CHIEF PHARISEE)

You're right. For the time being, we must not let anyone know that it is with us. We shall introduce it with dramatic fervor to the public after the dust settles. There will be a mad rush to kiss it and make offerings.

ANANYAS (HIGH PRIEST)

While you sit here and salivate about the money coming your way, his disciples will make away with his body. That will be the end of your dreams and delusions.

He looks at the COMMANDER.

COMMANDER

Softly—

We must admit that our 'Hakeldama' plot has failed. It beats me that a nonentity like him could outstrip us.

ANANYAS (HIGH PRIEST)

That, too, getting straight to Pilate.

ELIAZAR (CHIEF PHARISEE)

What the hell is this all about? Who would want the body of a crucified man?

PRIEST

Who is so keen to get his carcass? What for?

COMMANDER

I remember hearing about a man called Joseph of Arimathea. Now, I have come to know that he is an eminent ship owner under the Roman Empire. He owns several mineral mines abroad. He is credited with a major role in the prosperity of the Roman Empire.

ANANYAS (HIGH PRIEST)

I have come to know that he introduced himself to Pilate as an ardent follower of Jesus. He has ready access to Pilate.

COMMANDER

In that case, there's nothing we could have done to prevent him from getting what he wanted. He is also known to be a deft magician and a sharp schemer.

ELIAZAR (CHIEF PHARISEE)

It would have been quite satisfying to claim that the latest Messiah also ended up being buried in Hakeldama among criminals. But that, too, failed.

Pause

Anything else to sort out?

ANANYAS (HIGH PRIEST)

Derisively—

No, no, we've gambled enough already. After all, he was hailed as the King of the Jews as he lay on the cross. He should be given a royal burial. Or else it will reflect badly on us.

ALL burst out into laughter.

COMMANDER

Frankly, we haven't done too badly, either. I didn't expect our playbook to hold so well and help avoid bloodshed. Let's hope it ends well.

PHARISEE

What happened to his numerous disciples and followers? Belying our fears, none has shown up or put up a resistance.

ELIAZAR (CHIEF PHARISEE)

They fled for their life and hid themselves out of sight. What else could you expect from fishermen? Courage has no role to play in their profession. They gather the fish that get into their nets, that's all. No chasing or killing is required, unlike in hunting.

ANANYAS (HIGH PRIEST)

It's wrong to say that those who battle against whales and surging waves have no courage. This Messiah impressed them as a shrewd man and a supreme magician.

In ridicule—

Pathetic poltroons. Obviously, they expected he would save himself and wouldn't need their help. They were sincerely expecting him to work a miracle to save himself. When that didn't happen, they panicked and fled. None of them dare anymore to much as mention his name—poor, hapless guys. We should gift some nets and boats to help them make a living when we meet them.

EVERYONE laughs.

COMMANDER

We have come to know that the dead Nazarene has some secret disciples. We will catch them soon.

ANANYAS (HIGH PRIEST)

Thanks to the good thinking and hard work you and Phinahas put in,
a likely disaster has been averted. The people got a man to crucify.
The Roman Empire will continue in its imperial glory to the end of
times... and hopefully our priesthood too.

PRIEST

You are quite right; hard work alone would not have sufficed to
succeed in this task. A sharp mind as well was needed. In any case, a
sinister chapter is now ending. We can, at last, celebrate the Passover
peacefully.

ALL exit.

SCENE 9

PETER walks in alone. He stands at the center of the stage. Looks scared as he glances this way and that.

JOHN, his head fully covered, enters from the dark side of the stage. On seeing PETER, he uncovers his head and reveals his face.

PETER

Softly—

Why are you wandering around aimlessly like this?

JOHN

I know I have a long time ahead. Besides, no one will believe I have become his disciple at so tender an age.

PETER

How come you have become so articulate suddenly?

JOHN

The master has bestowed knowledge and wisdom on me
abundantly.

PETER

You have seen the master as he lay nailed to the cross. But how can
you claim that he spoke to you? What is the special wisdom you got
from the master beyond what we have?

JOHN

There is a communion that transcends words and syllables—a sort
of oneness between two souls—the soul of the crucified master
imparted the wisdom of it to me.

PETER

Why wasn't I favored?

JOHN

Worldly weakness made you, Cephas. Betray the master thrice. You
were the first to understand him as the Son of the living God. Yet,
when it really mattered, you failed.

PETER

Startled—

What makes you think so?

JOHN

I was there then beside you. No divination was needed.

PETER

I hear that when our master died on the cross, the veil of the temple was torn in two; the dead were quickened, and they came out of the tombs.

JOHN

As the master said, no one need anymore to worship in fear and in secrecy. The tearing of the veil set that change in motion. The priesthood of Moses was meant to last only till the coming of the Messiah. Melchizedek's heavenly priesthood has now dawned. Preaching the message of love unto the ends of the earth is the godly mission enjoined on us as his disciples.

PETER

Unimaginable is the cruelty perpetrated by the Roman Empire. How long more will we, the elect of Yahweh, bear this crushing slavery? I long to see the end of this empire, but there is no indication that it will happen in my lifetime. Do not let me die with my wish unfulfilled, Lord.

JOHN

This nightmare of cruelty will soon come to an end. God will send down on the rulers of Rome both insanity and the pleasures of life beyond measure. Dysfunctional families, murders, and suicides will weaken its foundation. When the end of the empire stares Caesar in his face, he will build a new massive throne in its name.

PETER

Does that mean the Roman Empire will never end? Will this cruelty continue forever? I now believe that you have the power of divination. Tell me, what's the way forward for me who has denied the master?

JOHN

On you, who denied the master, Caesar's spirit will build a new empire. It will have thousands of temples and priests—all in your name. A new Roman Empire, a new establishment, will come into existence. Its boundaries will extend to the ends of the earth.

PETER

Startled—

What is this that I am hearing?! I am already guilty of denying the master thrice. Master, I cannot comprehend your ways. You appeared to that woman Mary after your resurrected and not to us. You made me deny you thrice. But if what you just said happens, it will be like denying him continuously till the end of history.

He casts a suspicious glance at John.

JOHN

When that mythological priesthood established in your name comes
to an end, the Messiah will descend among clouds in the company of
angels and preside over the final judgment. When the sun of
righteousness rises on the horizon, you shall know the day of his
coming has arrived.

After a brief pause, he approaches PETER.

Many have recognized you as a Galilean disciple of the master. If you
don't want anyone to recognize you, come with me. We still have a
lot to do. Let us go.

PETER

Where?

JOHN

I am going to a secure place.

PETER

Which secure place? Where on Earth can I find a secure place? The
doors of deliverance are closing against me.

JOHN

Why do you think so? I am going to the place where the woman of
Magdala lives.

PETER

What!

Derisively—

To the Queen of Sheeba?

JOHN

You can't find a place safer than that now. The Romans have a big
army and an efficient intelligence system, and they are everywhere.

PETER

Repentant—

I don't fear for my life anymore. I wish I had been crucified with him.

JOHN

There is something greater than that for you to do for the time being.
There is time for martyrdom yet. You'll surely attain it, God willing.

PETER looks dismayed hope at John.

JOHN

We have no time to lose. I also must search for Thomas.

He prepares to go.

PETER

Have you any idea where he is now?

JOHN

He is busy preparing for a long journey. He says the master was keen that he should undertake it.

PETER

Surprised—

The master mandated it! Can this be true? How foolish I was to think that I knew everything. I thought Thomas was just boasting.

JOHN

Taking a few steps—

He alone has truly known Christ. Thomas is destined for something great and unique.

Sorrowing—

Hardly anyone else has known Him as he is—he really is. That is the greatest injustice the master has suffered.

JOHN exists along with PETER.

SCENE 10

The ELIAZAR (CHIEF PHARISEE), ANANYAS (HIGH PRIEST), military COMMANDER, and ELIHU are on the stage. They are dressed as before. The CENTURION, likewise, enters. He appears fatigued and downcast.

COMMANDER

Buoyant—

Your absence has now been made up for.

ANANYAS (HIGH PRIEST)

Studying the centurion with curious eyes—

What's gone wrong with him? He has come out victorious and lumbers like a defeated man.

ELIAZAR (CHIEF PHARISEE)

The lightning bolt seems to have struck him, too, beside the towers of the temple and the tall trees surrounding it. You, too, got stuck?

PRIEST

Taking a close look at the centurion—

His ears are still safe in their place.

ELIAZAR (CHIEF PHARISEE)

This time around, has someone cut off your tongue instead of your ears?

CENTURION

I... I am going back to my native place.

COMMANDER

You may go; nobody is stopping you. Thanks to you, the task assigned to us was accomplished smoothly. You will receive the rewards and titles from Caiaphas and Pilate that await you. Have a richly deserved long vacation. I shall recommend you for promotion and placement in Rome itself.

CENTURION

Humbly—

I don't set much store by rewards, promotions, and placements.

There are treasures thieves won't steal, and worms can't eat. They are heavenly. I am going to invest my treasures there.

ALL look at each other, confused.

COMMANDER

Your service is invaluable. Your intellect is superb, and your sense of duty commendable. I have recommended you for a big reward.

ELIAZAR (CHIEF PHARISEE)

Too much of intellectual brilliance can also be problematic. Would he have behaved like this otherwise?

ANANYAS (HIGH PRIEST)

Yelling in anger—

Malchus! Malchus!

Dumbstruck, ALL turn their eyes toward the ANANYAS (HIGH PRIEST).

CENTURION

Stammering after kneeling

Rabbuni... Rabbuini... Rabbuni...

ANANYAS (HIGH PRIEST)

How are your brother, Commander Michaes, and his son, Onesimos, keeping?

The CENTURION kneels. He removes the cap that signifies his authority and holds it in his hands.

ANANYAS (HIGH PRIEST)

I ransomed you and your brother from slavery. I gave you power and recognition. In return, I asked for your service only for the preservation of the Roman Empire.

After a pause, in a grave tone—

First, your brother took the side of the Nazarene through his son. And now you too.

CENTURION

He saved Onesimos while he was lying on his deathbed, Rabuni.

PRIEST

Now you too! Stop! Something terrible has happened to you. Whatever you built toiling long and hard has been shattered to the ground in a single night. What a tragedy! What an irony of fate!

ELIAZAR (CHIEF PHARISEE)

Along with an ear, you also must have lost a lot of blood. That seems to have ruined your mental balance. And then, you have also forfeited many coveted awards and rewards.

CENTURION

Draws his sword.

I am returning this sword. Nothing that is won by the sword is permanent. Every sword will always have another sword drawn against it. It will shed blood. This sword is stained by the blood of innumerable infants. If I continue to carry it, that stain will spread to my heart and my soul. I will never be able to clean it. I shall do penance for the crimes I have committed by submitting myself to their consequences.

ANANYAS (HIGH PRIEST)

In return for the ransom I paid, I demand your life and your brother's life and all you have pledged to me.

ELIHU THE PRIEST comes running and places his hand on the sword.

ELIHU (THE PRIEST)

Let this sword remain with me. Its stain shall not stick to me.

ELIAZAR (CHIEF PHARISEE)

You already have a previous stain on you. What can be worse than that?

PHARISEE

It is written that the priests have handed over their swords and arrows to King David's centurion. Just the opposite has happened here. A bad omen indeed!

MYSTERIOUS VOICE

The blood of babies—the blood of babies.

COMMANDER

The sword will not stand a priest in good stead.

ELIAZAR (CHIEF PHARISEE)

Why refuse something that is given for free? Beware of greed; it has no limit.

PRIEST

Whenever the Word fails, the sword will help me prevail.

CENTURION

Those who repose their faith in the sword shall fall by the sword. Only the message of love has lasting effectiveness. With this sword, I have massacred thousands of babies just to get rid of one baby—a sacrificial offering of babies—an unheard of sacrifice.

ANANYAS (HIGH PRIEST)

Sacrifices are pleasing to Yahweh. As per the order of Melchizedek, priests alone can offer them.

ELIAZAR (CHIEF PHARISEE)

Melchizedek's orders are aimed at getting a share of the offering. If ten out of ten falls into our lap, then all the praise and glory are exclusively ours. Nothing will be left for God then.

PHARISEE

Melchizedek, the king of Shalom, is known as the emperor of peace. How on Earth can you, who carries the sword, even pronounce his name?

PRIEST

Arrogantly—

Didn't Yahweh order boy Isaac to be offered in sacrifice? So, getting this sword stained by the blood of a few babies is no big deal. The preservation of the world requires that for a good cause, many lose their lives.

Holding aloft the sword after a pause—

The blood of many more will have to be offered in sacrifice for maintaining the integrity of the empire, and for the preservation of the temple.

CENTURION

Rome had foolishly thought that the destruction of the empire could be prevented by killing a baby. To secure the throne of Herod, I killed thousands of babies. Yet, one baby escaped. He now rules as king, as the redeemer of the world—as the monarch of the world.

COMMANDER AND ANANYAS (HIGH PRIEST)

Startled—

What! That baby escaped. He became a king.

CENTURION

Yes, indeed. He is the very man to whom you gave the title 'King of the Jews.' He is the king of kings, the only monarch, the Messiah—the only babe who escaped the war on babies.

COMMANDER, ELIAZAR (CHIEF PHARISEE), AND ANANYAS (HIGH PRIEST)

Dismayed—

King of kings? The Messiah? A crucified man owning a kingdom.? What the hell am I hearing?

ANANYAS (HIGH PRIEST)

Accursed is the man who dies hanging on a tree. Don't you know that?

PRIEST

He who is lifted up on the cross is condemned to the land of the dead.

CENTURION

His kingdom is not of this world. It is the power, the divine energy, that upholds the world. Even if the heavens and the earth disappear, the message of his love will stay as music to the dance of life.

MYSTERIOUS VOICE

The king of kings. The king of kings. The kingdom of love sustains everything. Love is life.

Light fades on the stage. The uproar of people is heard. The background music gets louder.

SCENE 11

Dim light falls on the stage. A distant view of the Jerusalem Temple is visible on the back curtain. The rising sun becomes visible on the horizon. A WOMAN, panting, scampers in from one side of the stage to the other in a palpable excitement and evident joy. MARY OF MAGDALENE looks sleep-starved.

MARY MAGDALENE

He has risen from the dead! Jesus of Nazareth has risen! Come and see! The tomb is empty!

JOHN and PETER come running. They look at her, puzzled.

MARY MAGDALENE

Paying scant attention to them—

Jesus of Nazareth has risen from the dead! Come, everyone, and see it for yourself!

She rushes to the door opposite. JOHN and PETER follow her.

SCENE 12

The stage is bare. The background music keeps rising and falling. After a while, JOHN rushes in, panting. He is followed by PETER.

Exhausted, PETER stops and takes a few deep breaths.

JOHN turns to PETER.

PETER

All this is beyond my comprehension. The tomb is empty. The stone with which the tomb was sealed is rolled away. The body of the Master isn't there in the cave.

JOHN

Didn't you hear what Mary said?

PETER

Looks incredulously at John.

But Lord, why don't you appear to us? Don't I daily praise and thank
you for not letting me be enslaved and for not letting me be born a
woman? Lord, you hailed me as Caiphas the rock and found me
steadfast and unwavering in my loyalty to you. Yet you show
yourself to her? How can this be? I find it hard to believe her.

JOHN

I believe her fully. I'm going away.

PETER

Where to?

JOHN

To Galilee... on the strength of Mary Magdalene's words... as the
Master had wanted.

PETER

It is true; no place is better than one's birthplace. I am leaving this
accursed city, Jerusalem, and heading straight for Galilee. Aren't the
others also headed there?

JOHN

We have nothing to do with Jerusalem anymore. The days of
priesthood are over. Pilgrims won't have to traverse mountains and
valleys to reach places of worship. As the Master said, the Jerusalem

Temple has become a den of thieves. God is not on this mountain or that mountain. God is where people live together in love and righteousness. We take to heart the exhortation of the master to worship God in spirit and in truth. Spread this message, taking it as a mission we have received.

PETER

Only after we get into the Sea of Galilee and struggle with its surging waves will we regain our old vigor and vitality—and the fish too. Thank goodness the nightmare is over, and a new dream begins.

JOHN

Turning back—

Oh Jerusalem, how our hearts are troubled by the thoughts about you, the fate that awaits you as prophesied by our master. You are bound to suffer the consequences of your corrupt practices. You reek of blood, the blood of the innocents. Old Jerusalem must make way for a new Jerusalem where peace and joy will embrace each other in an everlasting joy for mankind. God himself will then make His abode among the people. We shall go to Galilee. We shall meet Him there.

MYSTERIOUS VOICE

We will go to Galilee. We shall meet him there. We will go to Galilee. We shall meet him there. We shall meet him there.

JOHN and PETER exit.

THE END.

www.ingramcontent.com/pod-product-compliance
Lightning Source LLC
Chambersburg PA
CBHW021505090426
42739CB00007B/472